MY LOGICAL CONCLUSION

BY
SANDY MORIARTY

My Logical Conclusion
ISBN: 978-1-939570-74-1
Copyright © 2017 by Sandy Moriarty

Published by Word and Spirit Publishing
P.O. Box 701403
Tulsa, Oklahoma 74170
wordandspiritpublishing.com

ACKNOWLEDGMENTS

My inspiration comes from my husband, John, who pushes me to become all God has planned for me and not settle for anything less. My drive comes from my kids and knowing that, if they can do anything through Christ who strengthens them, so can I.

Thanks to my son, Mitchell, my encourager to my son, Jake, my abundance and to my daughter, Julia, my spice.

So many kisses go to my husband who believed in me and kept me moving throughout the writing process.

I love you all beyond any words I can express in writing.

MY LOGICAL MISSION

My mission is to bring God, our Father, and the words of the Bible, down from this far away place in Heaven and into a place where you can meet Him, hear Him and know Him and live with Kingdom purpose in mind. All of this is accomplished through a relationship with His son, Jesus Christ. God is my logical conclusion for every need and every situation, as well as, every good and holy blessing. I will strive to empower you, through the Holy Spirit, with biblical knowledge of the character and nature of God so that He becomes your logical conclusion for life and Jesus becomes your Lord.

2 PETER 1: 2-8

May grace and peace be multiplied to you through the knowledge of God and Jesus our Lord. His divine power has given us *everything* required for life and Godliness through the knowledge of Him who called us by His own glory and goodness. By these He has given us very great and precious promises, so that through them you may share in the divine nature, escaping the corruption that is in the world because of evil desires. For this very reason, make every effort to supplement your faith with goodness, goodness with knowledge, knowledge with self-control, self-control with endurance, endurance with Godliness, Godliness with brotherly affection, and brotherly affection with love. For if these qualities are yours and are increasing, they will keep you from being useless or unfruitful in the knowledge of our Lord Jesus Christ.

(HCSB, emphasis added)

INTRODUCTION

(Why is God "My Logical Conclusion")

Many years have passed since I was a first year law student praying to go unnoticed in the back of the class. It's ironic; while we discussed the doctrine of "separation of church and state" in law school… there was praying, lots and lots of praying, in the classroom. Not the right kind of praying; more like the frantic, last-minute begging, which led to deal making with God. You know the deals I'm talking about, right? *God, if you get me through this, today I will never* (fill in the blank, miss church again or drink too much again or eat too much again or whatever). I'm sure you have your version of "The Deal." Our deal went something like this: "God, if you get me out of this class today, I promise I won't go out partying, and I will be prepared tomorrow." I would call that scenario Contract Law 101, which happens to be a first year law class and probably the class for which I was making the deal.

Most law professors prefer the Socratic Method to extract information from students in order to teach legal concepts. This method takes its name from the Greek Philosopher, Socrates, and is designed to stimulate critical thinking and ideas based on a series of questions— pointed, relentless questions, I might add. As law students, even when "totally" prepared, the brutality of these questions left us feeling attacked and usually like complete idiots. So, most of the time, I, along with my fellow classmates, sat quietly, attempting to duck and hide behind our rather large law books and each other, hoping and, yes, praying that each day the bombardment would not fall upon us. Once someone else's name was called, we all quietly cheered and secretly thanked God. Unfortunately, our names were on the professor's list, and, despite our attempts, we never escaped the interrogation.

The cases we read and prepared, daily presented a system of merging a fact scenario with legal statutes and judicial analysis. This system taught us to extract the important information and discard the irrelevant fluff.

You may be wondering about the relevancy of law school and my law degree to this book about God. Well, as a lawyer, I can't help but use my background when reading the Bible and praying. More importantly, I am certain God has always intended that I utilize my legal training to stimulate critical thinking and ideas in order to merge facts from my life with His Word. For me, petitioning God and petitioning the court are two processes that are very similar. Dissecting a Scripture and presenting it to God is very much the same as dissecting a statute and petitioning the court. In Psalm 5:3, David says he pleads his case to the Lord and watches expectantly. David knew that he could find justice in the Lord's court.

This paragraph has some relevant definitions and interesting statistics so bear with me. I googled "meaning of Bible" just to see what I would find on the internet. I learned that the Bible was believed to be written over a period of 1,700 years by over 40 authors from different backgrounds. Its origin derives from Hebrew which was later translated into Latin and Greek. The word "Bible" originated from the Greek word "biblia" which means books. In the 13th century, "books" was shortened to book, i.e. "Bible." The Bible is a compilation of divinely inspired holy texts or scripts, thus the term Scripture developed. One source touts that over five billion copies have sold and the Bible is considered to be the best-selling book of all time. It has been read by more people and been translated into more languages than any other book. Over the years, this collection of "holy books," which is believed to be God's Word, has become the source of Christian teaching worldwide.

Merriam-Webster defines Scripture as the books of the Bible; a body of writings considered sacred and authoritative. *Black's Law Dictionary* is a tool that all first year law students purchase to gain basic knowledge of legal terms from "Abandon" to "Zoning" and everything in between. In this dictionary, the term "statute" is defined as a particular law enacted and established by the will of the legislature or department of government; the written will of the legislature that constitutes the law of the state. Logically, I began to compare the use of Scriptures with statutes. I found their definitions similar: Scriptures are God's written authority and statutes are the government's written authority. Both are used to teach, protect, and implement the will of the governing body. There are, of course, some major differences in philosophy, but the idea of using laws and petitioning a higher Court for a ruling are much the same. While the Judge in our country's court system is not the creator of the universe who seeks to save the world, I do believe our court system was once modeled after biblical principles.

My mind visualizes our everyday trials in life much the same as a court case, and the Bible is full of Scripture's or statutes. For example, every court case has a main issue that has to be analyzed and presented to the judge for a ruling. There is almost always a rule of law or statute covering the main issue and a conclusion or summation that merges the issue and statute with the particular fact situation. In comparison, the journey we face in everyday life is filled with countless issues just like a court case. God's Scriptures become our legal statutes or laws. It is an easy leap to merge our life's journey with God's statutes and develop a summation or conclusion. This process allows me to build a case covering my fact situation and to apply God's own Word (or statutes, if you will) to present to His court. I am not talking about a step by step formula for solving problems. This system creates in us revelation knowledge of who we are in Christ gained through studying God's word.

There are so many advantages to God's court system, but what stands out for me is that God is the ultimate Judge and Jury, He never makes a mistake in His ruling and He is just. Sometimes, when God makes a ruling, we may wonder about or even doubt the outcome, but in the long run when we look back, we see God's wisdom.

> THERE ARE SO MANY ADVANTAGES TO GOD'S COURT SYSTEM, BUT WHAT STANDS OUT FOR ME IS THAT GOD IS THE ULTIMATE JUDGE AND JURY, HE NEVER MAKES A MISTAKE IN HIS RULING, AND HE IS JUST.

The Bible is filled with stories, promises, and prayers for us to use and rely on for a life of encouragement and victory. God sees His Word to completion in the form of promises and covenants. God's Word is truth that doesn't fail. In Luke 1:37, Luke writes that no Word from God will ever fail. In Isaiah 55:11, the Lord declares that His Word will achieve the purpose for which it was sent. God has kingdom purpose for us which is so much greater than we can imagine.

God is an intelligent, all knowing being. He has given us a divinely-inspired book that has passed the test of time. Many scholars, scientists, and archeologists have tried to disprove the existence of

Jesus only to prove that, statistically, there is more evidence to prove His existence than to disprove. I know this method sounds unemotional and cold, but I will strive to show you how the Holy Spirit infuses God's love, grace, and mercy into His organized structure. I believe God has called us to use our minds to logically think and test His principles and come to Him seeking a greater understanding of His power. If we can understand His Word, His Spirit will transform us and allow us to walk and live according to His higher purpose. Our cause will become His cause and we will be victorious every time—in God's timing and for God's glory.

Many of you may be asking, "Where is my faith in all of this logic?" Faith is defined as a belief in something for which there is no proof; complete trust. In Hebrews 11:1, Paul says that faith is the reality of what is hoped for, the proof of what is not seen. For my belief system to work, I rely heavily on my faith in the existence of God and that He created the universe. I also believe that God chose a few people, over the course of many years, and inspired them to share with the world the happenings in their lives and the miracles and the sorrows they witnessed along their way. One such happening was the life, death, and resurrection of Jesus, all of which we read about in the Bible. It is with great faith that I believe the events that these people transcribed thousands of years ago. I did not see any of these events; I have no proof of the occurrence of anything that happened in the Bible. I hope for what I cannot see. I now have witnessed, with my own eyes, happenings, events, and circumstances in my life that can only be described as miracles. These circumstances have no explanation except for divine intervention. These miracles strengthen my faith in a God that I cannot see. Faith in God and in His Word has become my only logical conclusion.

The Trinity refers to the Father, Son, and the Holy Spirit. The Bible speaks to this union of three-in-one in 1 John 5:7. Many times throughout the Bible God is called our Father, but in John 1:1 He is also called the Word. "The Word was made flesh and dwelt among us as the only begotten son (Jesus) of the Father" (John 1:14). In John 10:30, Jesus says that He and the Father are one. Jesus was sent by His Father to be the Savior of the world (see 1 John 4:14). The Holy Spirit is the Comforter, whom the Father sent in His name to teach us all things in remembrance of what Jesus taught to the disciples while He walked the earth (see John 14:26). In this book, I will be referring to God the Father; Jesus the Son, Lord, and Savior; and the Holy Spirit, who is the Comforter. They are one with three purposes commissioned for the work of our one Almighty God and Creator. I believe that Jesus is the Son of God and the Word of God made flesh in order to walk the earth to teach us the ways of our Father, God. His life, death, and resurrection were all necessary to clear the path of redemption for humanity. The Holy Spirit is God's gift for us to guide us and to allow revelation of the Word. Throughout this book, when I proclaim that God is my logical conclusion, I am speaking to the three-in-one Trinity as a unit.

This book is written from a legal slant. The title, *My Logical Conclusion*, sums up and simplifies my attempts at a more sophisticated title. The basic format or method used in each chapter is expressed through the JOURNEY, EXPLORING the STATUTES, and UNDERSTANDING the SUMMATION or what I developed as the JESUS METHOD. The *Journey* usually describes a story or experience that I have faced in my life where there was a conflict or trial that relates to the subject at hand. *Exploring the Statutes* sets forth a set of Scriptures that I will explore, and I will describe to you how they apply to the conflict. I have provided several Scriptures in each chapter. I hope that one or two of them speak to you and become your "go to" Scripture for future reference. Keep in mind that I don't have *all* of these

Scriptures memorized. Some I researched and learned as I wrote this book. Others have become my "go to" Scriptures over the years and I have committed to memory. *Understanding the Summation* merges the Journey with the Statutes and provides analysis that will lead you to a deeper understanding of God's character in order to logically conclude that God is sovereign and all powerful and, thus, resolves everything in life.

My logical conclusion is not based on mindless recitation of Scripture, but rather on my relationship with Jesus, the Savior, and on my faith in His Word. God's plan is designed for us to first know Him, love Him, and serve Him. It is not my premise that we throw God's Word at Him and demand a quick fix or ruling in our favor. My premise is for us to deepen our knowledge of the character and nature of God the Father, Jesus our Lord and Savior, and the Holy Spirit. We must learn that our lives revolvearound God and not His around us. Once we turn our focus to God, we begin to see the world through His eyes and to want what He wants. His Will becomes our will, and our quest to live a better life becomes one with godly intent, not worldly intent. Then, we begin to live with kingdom purpose and enjoy His many blessings. *That is my premise: to use the Word for kingdom purpose and eternal impact while getting to know Jesus deeper along the way.*

We must first meet the Savior and then learn His Word to know His deeper purpose. The JESUS METHOD, as used throughout this book, is designed to empower us with greater biblical knowledge and present the Word to our God in a logical fashion to achieve the kingdom purpose He has planned for us. In an effort to impart what God has taught me, and is still teaching me, about His character and nature, God inspired me to share my journey and my life experiences. As I wrote each story, I tried to be transparent and real. As you read each story, I pray that you hear God's voice, that you grow in your knowledge of Him, and that you delight in the law of the Lord. God is

my logical conclusion for everything. I pray my logical conclusion becomes yours.

PSALM 1: 1-2

Blessed is the man Who walks not in the counsel of the ungodly, Nor stands in the path of sinners, Nor sits in the seat of the scornful; But his delight *is* in the law of the LORD, And in His law he meditates day and night.

NKJV

PSALM 19: 7,8

The *Law* of the Lord is perfect, converting the soul;
The *Testimony* of the Lord is sure, making wise the simple;
The *Statutes* of the Lord are right, rejoicing the heart;
The *Commandment* of the Lord is pure, enlightening the eyes.

NKJV

MY PLAN

JOURNEY

There was a time in my life when I found myself unexpectedly out of work due to a down-turn in my industry. During this time, I made phone calls and attended business lunches. I sent out numerous resumes—frankly, more than I ever sent when I was a new hire fresh out of college looking for my first job. I put ads in legal magazines. Daily, I checked my email inbox looking for a reply. I didn't receive much interest from all of my effort. I have always been a pretty faithful person; I pray, I have a daily devotion (most of the time), I diligently tithe (without fail), and I donate to worthy causes. So why was this happening to me? Why was I lying in bed eating chocolate with the cat, waiting, wondering, and asking, "Why is *my* plan not working?"

Okay, I only spent a couple of days in bed watching old movies with the cat, and it was raining one of those days. It's okay to watch movies in bed on rainy days, right? At least, I began each day with a devotion and prayer time. When I was working, I had a much shorter prayer and devotion time. Not working had definitely afforded me more time to really pray, research, and talk to God. I knew this time at home was the perfect opportunity to grow spiritually.

I was enjoying this time with God, but every day when I finished my prayers I found myself bored. Moreover, I found myself battling in my mind with frustration and confusion about what to do next. Yes, I was even angry. I couldn't believe I was facing a job/career change. I didn't have an answer for why this job hunt was taking so long. I have a college degree and this big law degree...this layoff at home was not part of my plan.

I'm the kind of person who likes to know the plan. I usually develop the plan. I was very good at planning. Most of my life, I made plans and then asked God to, please, please, please, bless my plans and make it all work out nice and neat. Idle time is uncomfortable for me; it is not my friend. I'm not really a clean freak, but I did spend some of my days cleaning out closets and drawers. That only lasted so long—I only had so many closets.

I just wanted answers to some big questions: "What was I supposed to do now?" "Should I start my own business within my field?" "Should I re-invent myself *completely?*" So, there I was facing major life-changes in my early fifties. Really, God? REALLY? I mean, how smart was it to stop using a degree that took seven years to obtain and had the potential to earn six figures?

Well, my phone wasn't ringing. My plan wasn't working. Yes, I was praying and spending extra time with God, but I wasn't really quieting myself and listening.

I remembered that several years ago, I heard a pastor preach about having his suitcase packed. He was talking about the concept of being ready for the next step. In his early years, he was not making progress toward his goals until he began preparing properly (i.e. "packing his bags" properly). He began taking steps to make his dreams a reality instead of waiting for something to drop in his lap.

Okay, so what did that mean for me?

You scholars of history might be familiar with John F. Kennedy's famous line from his 1961 inaugural address where he said, "Ask not what your country can do for you, rather, ask what you can do for your country." I use this quote to illustrate a paradigm shift I was forced to make in my life. This same quote can and should be used with a godly purpose in mind.

I changed the quote to read, "Ask not what God can do for you, rather, ask what you can do for God."

For years, I had been using my writing skills in my work. As I thought back over my career and my life, I remember that my writing abilities date back to high school and college when I scored very high in all of my writing composition classes. While my degree wasn't a writing degree, I knew I had a natural inclination toward communication using the written word. I had been explaining legal issues to clients on a daily basis in written legal opinions for years.

So, while asking these big questions and wondering what to do next, I was hearing God's still, small voice saying, "Get out of bed and go write something." However, at the same time, I was also hearing another voice saying, "I have no idea what to write. Should I write a blog or a book? Who would publish my book? How do I even write a blog? Who will read what I have to write? Why would anyone listen to me? People will know too much about my personal life…" et cetera. When I finally slowed down long enough to silence all the thoughts in my head, I heard God say, "I have been giving you ideas for years, just start writing."

This was well and good, but in my everyday life, I still wanted to be in *control*. Funny thing—so did God. I still wanted to develop all of the plans for my life. So did God. I wanted to know the one-year plan for the future, the five-year plan, the ten-year plan, and the twenty-five year plan. Can you say "Control Freak"? Where was my faith?

His Word says that He knows all of the plans. It doesn't say that Sandy knows all the plans or that He is going to *tell* me all the plans. As much as I hated to admit it, I was not omniscient or all knowing…God was and is. I could not see into the future, and I don't know the plan for tomorrow, much less a year from now or twenty-five years from now. I had tried to make plans for my career, but circumstances changed and my plans disintegrated time and time again. I was the one who was supposed to have it all together, and the thought of letting anyone see me out of control was hard to bear.

Finally, I had to let it go. I realized that I was exhausted trying to control it all. Moreover, relying on someone who is "all knowing" really made the most sense. I stopped searching for jobs and sending out resumes. I stopped making plans and asking God to bless them. I began asking God what He wanted me to do and how I could help in *His* plan. I began asking not what God could do for me, but, rather, what could I do for Him.

> I REALIZED THAT I WAS EXHAUSTED TRYING TO CONTROL IT ALL. MOREOVER, RELYING ON SOMEONE WHO IS "ALL KNOWING" REALLY MADE THE MOST SENSE… I BEGAN ASKING NOT WHAT GOD COULD DO FOR ME, BUT, RATHER, WHAT COULD I DO FOR HIM.

EXPLORING the STATUTES

1 John 3:20 – "God knows all things." (HCSB)

Jeremiah 29:11-14 – "For I know the plans I have for you"—this is the LORD's declaration—"plans for your welfare, not for disaster, to give you a future and a hope. You will call to Me and come and pray to Me, and I will listen to you. You will seek Me and find Me when you search for Me with all your heart. I will be found by you." (HCSB)

Psalm 116:6 – "The Lord guards the inexperienced; I was helpless; and He saved me." (HCSB)

Proverbs 21:5 – "The plans of the diligent lead surely to abundance and advantage." AMP

Psalm 32:8 – "I will instruct you and show you the way to go; with My eye on you, I will give counsel." (HCSB)

Psalm 139:13, 16 "For God created my inmost being… All the days ordained for me were written in your book before one of them came to be." (NIV)

Habakkuk 2:2 – "Write down this vision; clearly inscribe it on tablets so one may easily read it." (HCSB)

See also – Romans 8:31-32, Colossians 1:10, Psalm 119:105, Genesis 28:15, and Ephesians 1-9-10.

UNDERSTANDING the SUMMATION

One day, I did get out of bed. I sat at the computer and began writing devotions using stories and Scriptures that were familiar to me. The words just began to flow. I noticed that some of my *bags* were already packed. A most profound revelation occurred. The stories I was telling were from my life experiences. For years, I had been teaching my kids and myself some of these same Scriptures and Biblical principles that I was now implementing in this Jesus method. I had also been writing and leading a women's Bible study using some of these same writing skills. I was putting into action some of the ideas that were floating around in my head, but really nothing was new. God was behind the scenes of my life setting these plans into motion all along. Could it be that God had been planning for me to write from the beginning? Could it be that it was finally time to make God's plan *my plan?*

In reality, I had no idea what was going to come of these actions, but I knew that not trying would leave me helpless and unfulfilled. In Psalm 116:6, we read that the Lord guards the inexperienced. One of my favorite Scriptures is Proverbs 21:5, which says the plans of the diligent lead to abundance and advantage. Lying in bed with the cat and a bag of chocolate until 3:00 in the afternoon was NOT diligent. I couldn't expect abundance or advantage.

I certainly was NOT helpless, and He could save me from my confusion and doubts about the book. These ideas and talents all came from Him, and He would use them according to His plan for my future but for His glory not mine. The Lord declared a future of hope for me and not disaster. I began to realize that the disaster would come only if I continued to push for a plan that was not ordained by God. The disaster might have been my getting hired by one of those companies and never following that still, small voice prompting me to get out of bed and write *this book.*

Telling you about my writing skills was not an effort to boast or brag. I told you about these skills and about how they date back even to high school to show you that God built these talents into the inner most part of my being (see Psalm 139:13, 16). To answer my earlier question, yes, God had plans to use these writing talents for His purpose from the moment time began.

He has done the same for you!

I believe that God has uniquely designed each of us for a specific purpose. I challenge you to look inside yourself. Think about what you enjoy and what comes naturally for you. God is going to use what He has placed in you from the beginning. God has been equipping you for years. He, now, awaits your arrival into His plan.

You probably feel a peace and joy when you work in certain areas or perform certain tasks. Maybe you can teach, or use your hands to build or design clothes or jewelry. Maybe you have great organizational skills or create beautiful websites or work with kids. Maybe you can write stories or music or sing. People probably tell you all the time how talented you are at a particular skill. I have a friend who can decorate houses, another who can knit, and another who can draw. Whatever your talents, God can show you how to take these skills and turn them into good, fulfilling work for His kingdom.

If you are searching for God's plan for your life, *plan* to spend some time in prayer every day. Sit quietly and listen to that still, small voice inside that encourages you. Cast out the voice of discouragement and doubt that says you are inexperienced and will surely fail. Focus on God's statutes.

What does His Word say about you and your situation? Speak, out loud, Jeremiah 29:11 every day and know that God has a plan for you of hope for a future. Speak Psalm 32:8, which says that God will instruct you and show you the way to go; He has his eye on you, and He will give you counsel and the plans of the diligent will lead to abundance and advantage. Confess Proverbs 21:5.

Boldly go to God speaking these statutes/Scriptures believing that He will show you the way, and diligently look and listen for His plan to unfold. According to God's statutes, it is only logical to conclude that God created you and His plan for you before you were born. God has His eye on you and will instruct you and lead you to abundance and advantage if you diligently seek Him.

Begin to thank Him for the plan He has for your life and the gifts He has placed within you. Be ready to move forward with His plan and to make *His* plan *your* plan. If you hear that voice in your head telling you to get up and do something, then get up and do it. While you're waiting, if you have some ideas or a dream floating around in your head, write them down. In Habakkuk 2:2 we learn to write down our vision. Begin to ask God what you can do for Him every day to become part of His plan. When we are working within God's plan, we will feel His peace. It is up to Him to instruct and counsel and work out the details. God knows the plan He has for you, for your welfare and not for disaster. You have to take the first step. I'm excited for you and praying for you.

I pray that you "plan" to daily read the Word and spend time with Jesus in prayer. I also pray that you relinquish control and let God instruct you on the way you should go. I pray that you will be still and begin to hear God's plan for your life and be ready and willing to fulfill His vision, in Jesus' name, Amen.

God is...my logical conclusion for my plan.
Who is your plan?

Notes

Notes

MY HEAVENLY FATHER

JOURNEY

I have lived most of my life without my earthly father. My father died of a heart attack in his sleep when I was twenty years old. I remember the day quite vividly. It was the fall of my junior year of college when I found myself without a father. As the days and months passed, I would dream about him. (I guess it was him.) It looked like him from the back, but in my dreams I could never get close enough to touch him or see his face before I would wake up. Those dreams eventually faded, and the passage of time allowed me to dwell less and less on the loss of his presence in my life.

I moved on, completed college, and attended law school. While in law school, I began studying constitutional law and the Bill of Rights. I learned that as a citizen of this country, we as Americans have rights. Moreover, Thomas Jefferson wrote in The Declaration of Independence that we have certain inalienable rights, including life, liberty, and the pursuit of happiness. Merriam-Webster defines inalienable as impossible to take away or give up. No government or legal power can take these rights away.

Years ago, I began making a connection between viewing our rights as a "Christian citizen" in the same way as viewing our rights as an American citizen. While I was still in the early phase of my theory, I posed this question to several different people: "What rights do we have in Christ?"

I can't remember the exact words, but I was told something like… "We don't have rights. We are to follow God's commands and do what He tells us." As you can imagine, I was perplexed, dissatisfied and even a bit angry with that answer. Maybe I didn't ask the question properly to get the proper response. I am not sure what I expected to hear, but maybe something about love and Jesus.

However, it is probably better that I received such harsh feedback, since those answers fueled my discontent. As a result, those answers also propelled me into my own research project, where I soon found some wonderful and very powerful information on the subject of rights—not the Bill of Rights but rather what I now call the Bible of Rights.

EXPLORING the STATUTES

Galatians 4:1-7 – "What I am saying is that as long as an heir is under-age, he is no different from a slave, although he owns the whole estate. The heir is subject to guardians and trustees until the time set by his father. So also, when we were underage, we were in slavery under the elemental spiritual forces of the world. But when the set time had fully come, God sent his Son, born of a woman, born under the law, to redeem those under the law, that we might receive adoption to sonship.

Because you are his sons, God sent the Spirit of his Son into our hearts, the Spirit who calls out, "Abba, Father." So you are no longer a slave, but God's child; and since you are his child, God has made you also an heir."

John 1:12, 13 – "Yet to all who did receive him, to those who believed in His name, he gave the right to become children of God – children born not of natural descent, nor of human decision or a husband's will, but born of God." (NIV)

Philippians 3:20 – "Our citizenship is in Heaven and we eagerly await a Savior from there, the Lord Jesus Christ." (NIV)

Psalm 139:13 – "For you created my inmost being; you knit me together in my mother's womb." (NIV)

Romans 8:17 – "Now, if we are children, then we are heirs- heirs of God and co-heirs with Christ, if indeed we share in his sufferings in order that we may also share in his glory." (NIV)

Ephesians 2:6, 7 – "God raised us up with Christ and seated us with him in the heavenly realms in Christ Jesus, in order that in the coming ages, He might show the incomparable riches of his grace expressed in his kindness to us in Christ Jesus." (NIV)

See also – Galatians 5:22, 1 Peter 2:9

Definitions from *Black's Law Dictionary*, Abridged Fifth Edition, by Henry Campbell Black, M. A.

Adoption – Legal process pursuant to state statute in which a child's legal rights and duties toward his natural parents are terminated and similar rights and duties toward his adoptive parents are substituted. To take into one's family the child of another and give him or her all rights, privileges and duties of a child and heir.

Heir – There are many definitions of heirs in the dictionary – Heirs by Adoption – an adopted child takes all the rights of succession to property (if there is no Last Will & Testament) as those of a natural born child unless contrary intention is expressed in a Will.

UNDERSTANDING the SUMMATION

My research led me to Galatians 4:1-7, but mainly verses four through seven, which are in the Scriptures above. First, God showed me the word "Abba," which means Father. These verses tell us that God sent His Son, born under the law to redeem us from the law. Now we are adopted children with the Spirit of His Son in our hearts calling out "Abba, Father." We are God's children, and as such, His heirs.

When I read these words, I was in complete and total awe of God's almighty greatness. God took the time to speak to me; He answered pointed questions that I had asked earlier in life about rights in Christ. God had just revealed Himself and authenticated His presence in my life. I knew He was speaking directly to me and to my desire to know my rights in Him. He knew I had questions about "rights" in Christ and citizenship, but He parlayed that into heirship and adoption.

He also knew that I had been without a father for many years. That was not particularly on my radar at the time, but it was relevant to my life. Moreover, He answered my questions in terms that I understood all too well—legal terms. Adoption and heirship are legal terms that I had studied in law school. I had prepared wills for people and used those terms. At that point in my spiritual walk, I had no idea that those terms were in the Bible. I had no idea that the Bible could be used like a set of statutes in order to petition the Almighty Judge for support, protection, and blessings. This new information was a great revelation about God's justice system.

I was overwhelmed at how God was answering the questions that I posed to my friends. He had me; He taught me. I was all in and sold-out. That is the power of God's Word. It speaks to us where we are, when we need it.

At the same time, God showed me that He is my heavenly Father. I have since discovered Psalm 139:13, which states that God created my innermost being and knit me together in my mother's womb. Think on that verse for a moment; that is our heavenly Father. I don't knit, but I have watched others. It is a hands-on, eyes-on, attention-to-detail process and very time consuming. Our Father did that for each one of us in our mother's womb. He took the time to weave together every detail of our being, carefully choosing each one of our characteristics.

My earthly Dad was a fireman, but on his days home from the fire department, he was a carpenter. I would watch him measure and cut lumber. He would pay close attention to every detail to ensure that all the pieces fit like a puzzle. I can picture our Heavenly Father working on us in just the same manner. He crafted our every fiber and knows the number of hairs on our heads!

The Scriptures talk about our belief and confession in Jesus as our Lord, securing our citizenship in Heaven and we have the "right" to be adopted children of God and heirs with Christ to share in His glory. What do we share with Christ? What is our inheritance? What if you already have a father? I am going to address the former of the three questions first. I believe that these Scriptures spoke to me because my Dad passed away, and I needed that fatherly connection. God knew the time was perfect to teach me a two-fold lesson on using the rights we gain in Christ through adoption and heirship to reveal himself as my Heavenly Father. He didn't become my Father after or because my biological father died. God is not only a Father to those who are without; as you can see from Psalm 139, He has been there for everyone from the beginning in our mother's womb. He was our Father in the beginning, He is our Father now, and He will be our Father always. He is for everyone.

To answer the questions about our inheritance, I want to examine the legal definitions of adoption and heir from *Black's Law Dictionary* I included for you on pages 11-12. The first sentence in the definition of adoption speaks to terminating the rights of our natural parents and substituting the rights of our adoptive parents. In the world we live, that is the procedure for adopting a child. The rights of natural parents must be terminated before a child is eligible for adoption by new parents.

In God's kingdom, Galatians 4:1-7 is one of the Scriptures that allows us to terminate our spiritual rights to our parents in order terminate generational curses like the spirit of addiction and disease. We can be free of all of those curses that have plagued our families from generation to generation—alcoholism, cancer, abuse, mental illness, and more. Those family strongholds can be broken! When we begin claiming our new bloodline and our rights as adopted children of God, we are free from the strongholds of the past.

If we move to the second sentence of the adoption definition, which speaks to the child of another being given the rights, privileges, and duties of a child and heir, then we can see that an adopted child gains equality with a natural born child.

The definition of heir supports the idea of equality, for inheritance purposes, among adopted children and natural born children. Therefore, and this is a big therefore, everything that Jesus can do and everything that Jesus can access, as adopted children of God, we have equal authority to do and to access.

This is what we share with Christ. I ask you again to ponder that statement for a moment. Because we've been made heirs to the throne by Jesus Christ, we now share in and have access to all of God's power and resources, but most importantly we now inherit the kingdom of God. Jesus has the right to access God's power any time. He is seated at God's right hand. Jesus can heal the sick, calm storms, and raise the dead. We have full access to the Holy Spirit, who provides love, joy, peace, gentleness, faithfulness, patience, goodness, kindness, and self-control. We are citizens of the Kingdom of Heaven along with Jesus, the Son of God. Our Heavenly Father is the King of kings; we are royalty. Scriptures say that together with Christ we are seated in the heavens and that in the coming ages He will show us the incomparable riches of His grace through His kindness to us in Christ Jesus (see Ephesians 2:6-7).

However, with this great power comes great responsibility. Jesus used His power for one purpose: to advance the will of His Father. This is not *our* power; it is God's power channeled through us. It is similar to how we have access to the resources of our earthly father. I liken it to how the President's kids get to ride on Air Force One, but only because their dad is the President. They only have access to Air Force One because they are heirs to their father, the President.

We must utilize the vast magnitude of the power behind our authority. Our mission and the purpose for the great power entrusted to us is to work together with Christ to advance our Father's kingdom, not our own. We should be striving to change the world around us and make more heirs. I believe there are two dynamics to this:

First, we have to realize our place as royalty—our place as co-heirs to the throne and as brothers and sisters to the son of God. That's who we are, not the divorced, not the sick, not the worried, not the alcoholic, not the depressed, and not the addict. Those may be the attacks coming at us, but that's not who we *are*. We are children of the Most High God, the Creator of the Universe. As such we have access to His power and

His resources to change our circumstances. It's only logical to conclude that we start acting like royalty instead of peasants.

> FIRST, WE HAVE TO REALIZE OUR PLACE AS ROYALTY—OUR PLACE AS CO-HEIRS TO THE THRONE AND AS BROTHERS AND SISTERS TO THE SON OF GOD.

Second, we have to believe that we are saved, healed, and protected. Through God's power in us and for His glory, we have to believe that we are capable of accomplishing great tasks and, yes, even capable of walking on water like Peter and healing the sick like Jesus. (See Matthew 14:29 and Matthew 12:22) We have to believe that miracles are possible through our faith in Jesus Christ.

I pray that you will claim your bloodline as a child of God and your seat in heaven. View yourself as an heir to the throne of your Father, the King. Embrace your "rights" in Christ and your citizenship in heaven.

God is...my logical conclusion for my heavenly Father.
Do you know your heavenly Father?

Notes

Notes

MY PEACE

JOURNEY

"I really do want world peace," Sandra Bullock's character, Gracie, from *Miss Congeniality*, admitted as she flapped her hands over her crying eyes. Deep down, isn't that what we all want?

Or is it? Sure, I would like to live in a peaceful world where there is no fighting and nations are at peace. In America, we are so fortunate to live in a nation where many very brave soldiers are willing to die to ensure the peace of this great nation and all who live here! I don't take that lightly, and I am beyond thankful. However, what I sit and contemplate over coffee with my friends isn't world peace, or even how to solve the world's battles. Mostly, the issues we discuss are the everyday battles that shatter our "inner" world peace right here at home. So, I guess I would rephrase Gracie's statement to, "I really do want *inner* world peace."

I am going to take you back to the past quite a bit and walk you through some events that shape my peace story. My childhood went smoothly; no major catastrophes. The first dent in my peace armor occurred when I was a teenager. I played basketball, and I was a good little ball handler. The coach told me in front of the entire team that I would make the All-State team as a sophomore in high school. I had dreams of college ball…and then the unthinkable happened for a basketball player. I tore my left ACL!

The ACL or anterior cruciate ligament is the ligament in the inner knee that is used to help stabilize the leg. In the 1980s, the technology was not as advanced as it is today. At the time, I still had an inch to grow, and the repair surgery could hinder my growth resulting in my left leg forever remaining an inch shorter than the other. At this point, my ligament was not torn completely. I could still walk, but the next injury could be worse. I was faced with a choice: play basketball and risk another injury requiring the surgery…or quit basketball.

For me, this was not just quitting a game; it was making a decision to give up on my life-long dream. I loved basketball and my teammates. I had played since the fourth grade with a few of these girls. We had won some championships together. I must have been sixteen years old when I walked into the coach's office with tears streaming down my face and handed him my jersey—a varsity jersey I earned as a sophomore. I was crushed.

This is a day that shattered my peace.

The next dent came soon after I headed off to college to begin my junior year. It was early in September of 1984. I had just returned from Labor Day weekend at the lake instead of going home for a visit. I was twenty years old, and life was good. It was a beautiful late summer evening, and I was attending a night class on my college campus when my roommate's sister came into the classroom and asked me to come with her. I was told to call home, which was an hour and a half drive from my college. We had no mobile phones at the time.

On the short drive back to my college house, I was terrified. You can imagine all the scenarios playing in my mind. I remember the phone call—neither of my parents answered…gulp! The person on the other end of the call said, "Hold on while I get your mom." I thought to myself, "Mom is okay." I stood in my bedroom facing my bed, waiting for her to get on the line.

She spoke these words: "Your dad had a heart attack today in his sleep and he never woke up." With tears streaming down my face, I sank to the floor wishing desperately that I had spent the weekend with my Dad instead of friends at the lake.

This is a day that shattered my peace.

This next dent hit harder than even the other two. I would say that it shattered my *world*. In the mid 1990s my husband, John, and I had our first child. Everything was perfect. I had a good amount of morning sickness, and the doctor even used the word "text book" pregnancy. Up to this point, things were going our way, and our plans were working. I got pregnant again, and again I had morning sickness just like before. I went in for a normal check-up with a sonogram. This doctor routinely performed an early sonogram; we saw the heart beat and everything looked fine. However, the doctor said the size of the baby appeared small based on the number of weeks pregnant. He wanted us to come back in a few weeks to have another sonogram. The doctor did not appear concerned. We went on with our lives not knowing how our lives were about to change.

A few weeks passed, I was about nine weeks pregnant, and John and I were excited to go back for our next sonogram to see the baby. However, the sonogram technician was taking a really long time analyzing the screen and moving the device. We could see the perplexed look on her face, and finally she left the room. Our bliss was about to turn to heartbreak. The nurse came and asked us to sit in the doctor's private office. We listened as our doctor told us that there was no longer a heartbeat. He kept talking, but I'm not sure what he said. We were stunned. With tears streaming down my face, my husband drove me home.

This is a day that most definitely shattered my peace.

EXPLORING the STATUTES

2 Timothy 1:7 – "For God has not given us a spirit of fearfulness, but one of power, love and sound judgment." (HCSB)

Isaiah 41:10 – "Do not fear, for I am with you; do not be afraid, for I am your God. I will strengthen you; I will help you; I will hold on to you with My righteous right hand." (HCSB)

John 16:33 – "In Me you may have peace. In this world, you will have trouble, but take heart, I (Jesus) have overcome the world." (NIV)

Philippians 4:6, 7 – "Do not be anxious about anything but in every situation, by prayer and petition, with thanksgiving, present your requests to God. And the peace of God, which transcends all understanding, will guard your hearts and your minds in Christ Jesus." (NIV)

See also – Philippians 4: 6-7, Psalm 29:11, Psalm 118:6, Hebrews 13:6

UNDERSTANDING the SUMMATION

We live in a world where the devil is constantly throwing darts at us. He is looking to dent our armor so much so that it shatters our inner world peace. When our peace is shattered, we live in fear. Fear of what will happen next weakens us. Then we become ineffective, paralyzed, and defeated. When we live like that, the enemy has won.

So, how do we live each day in peace and not dread the unknown? How do we keep fear of what might happen from stealing our joy and robbing our peace? How do we defeat fear? Fear is the enemy of faith. The two emotions cannot occupy our mind at the same time. Our brain works like a computer's word processor, so treat it in similar fashion. We must select the "Find and Replace" button in our mind, fill in the blanks to "find" all the fear and worry words and sentences and "replace" them with Jesus' faith words and sentences. By uniting God's Word with our daily journey, we strengthen our armor. We replace the fear with the Word. When we recite God's statutes out loud, fear and dread weaken and our peace grows stronger. Knowing God's Word is the key to claiming the peace that God intends for our lives.

> BY UNITING GOD'S WORD WITH OUR DAILY JOURNEY, WE STRENGTHEN OUR ARMOR. WE REPLACE THE FEAR WITH THE WORD. WHEN WE RECITE GOD'S STATUTES OUT LOUD, FEAR AND DREAD WEAKEN AND OUR PEACE GROWS STRONGER.

In Isaiah 41:10 God says, "So do not fear, for I am with you; do not be afraid, for I am your God. I will strengthen you and help you; I will hold on to you with My righteous right hand." In John 16:33, we read that we will have trouble in this world. As Christians, we have *not* been promised a life free from trouble. In fact, if you are following God's commands and living for Him, I believe that your life will be filled with many attacks. Because the devil doesn't want you to win, he sends you minor setbacks that eventually lead to major setbacks.

Earlier I mentioned the fiery darts that cause the big dents or the armor shattering dents. Even now, I fight the daily smaller darts with thoughts that are constantly being downloaded in my brain and are trying to shatter my daily peace. I have a kid away at college and teenage drivers. In one day, I can get hit with a number of darts. "Mom, I lost my debit card…last night." "Mom, I got a 30% on a test (out of 100%)." "Mom, the computer won't work, and I can't do my homework." "Mom, smoke is filing the garage; I think it's my truck." The refrigerator is broken, the roof is leaking, and the company is laying off employees—the list can go on and on.

If I let myself dwell on my circumstances, my armor will weaken; fear and doubt will take over my thoughts. How many different thoughts go through your mind in five minutes—or even just one minute? We have negative thoughts about our jobs, our health, our kids, our spouses, and our finances all in matter of sixty seconds.

No one *wants* to live in fear. No one *wants* to dread what news might come with the next phone call or with the next day's events. But these thoughts about what could happen hold our inner peace hostage. So for inner peace, if I daily (strike that, hourly, or as necessary) replace those thoughts with the Word and dwell on God's promises, I am empowered and strengthened to endure whatever is thrown my way. I can't stop all of the attacks. Jesus tells us that in this world, we will have trouble. The enemy is going to keep throwing those darts. But Jesus also tells us that we can have peace because He has overcome the world.

I can change how I *react* to the darts. God's Word tells me not to be anxious, but to take my requests to Him and the peace that transcends all understanding will guard my heart and mind in Christ Jesus. That is a peaceful Scripture. My logical conclusion is that this peace in Christ Jesus transcends anything that I can work to attain on my own. Living according to God's "statutes" creates an impenetrable armor that guards my heart and mind and strengthens my peace shield. We can rise above our circumstances and live in God's peaceful realm.

I pray that you will daily recite Scriptures. Find the one that really speaks to you and download it to your memory and chose to replace the fear with faith. My favorites Scriptures are John 16:33, 2 Timothy 1:7, and Philippians 4:6-7.

God is...my logical conclusion for my peace.
Who is your peace?

Notes

MY LOVE

JOURNEY

I remember Friday nights when I was a teenager riding around in the car with friends singing along with the radio as loud as possible. Some of you might remember the old ballads from the 1980s rock bands. The so-called "love songs" sung by guys with long hair and leather pants. Those were the days of big hair for both guys and girls. As I was contemplating what to write for this chapter, many songs from the past and the present came to mind. Love is a very popular emotion when it comes to song lyrics. There are songs about first love, father-daughter love, long-lost love, and of course shattered love. There are songs about loving our dogs, loving our cars, and loving our country. There are even songs about a loving God.

One song from the 1980s spoke of love being a "second-hand emotion," and that lyric resonated with me. That phrase pretty much sums up how we treat the emotion of love. I am going to use the pronoun "we" because we all do this…we all take for granted the emotion that is tied to the word "love." We kind of throw that word around very nonchalantly. For me, I often say things such as I love to get up early and drink coffee and write. I love to go to breakfast with my friends. I also love to put on my PJs as soon as it gets dark outside (sometimes 6:00 p.m.). I love chocolate and watching old movies on rainy days. I love to watch college basketball. I loved our trip to Ireland we took as a family some years ago.

How many times did I say "love"? I could have gone on and on. Do I really "love" those things or just deeply like or enjoy them? Does the word "love" need to be associated with things or activities? If I walk up to you and say, "Oh, my gosh! I *love* your shirt," it makes a statement. You know I really like it. However, it's not quite as impressive if I say, "Oh, my gosh! I *enjoy* your shirt." After the weird look you give me, I quickly conclude that I won't be using that line again.

In contrast, I truly *love* my husband, my kids, and my extended family. I have some dear friends that I love. Most importantly, I love the Lord.

The same 1980s song also asked us who needs a heart when a heart it can be broken. That is a good question. We live in a society where who and what we love changes in an instant. My Google query, "songs with the word heartbreak in the title" yielded over 1.5 million songs. But that's just singing about it. The divorce rate is at an all-time high, which is amazing considering that many couples live together. People are opting to live together instead of marry, presumably, for fear that their marriage will fail and the relationship will end, thus leading to heartbreak and lost love.

Heartbreak can come in many forms such as the loss of a loved one from a tragic accident or from a senseless shooting. As I am writing today, my friends are heartbroken over the loss of their grandmother whose battle with a long-term disease came to an end. Let me tell you that they loved her—really loved her.

Whatever the case for loss, the song is right about one thing: the heart can be broken.

All that being said, have we watered down or diluted the effectiveness of the meaning of the word "love"? The word love is used so freely that when someone tells you they love you, do you believe them? Is there a love that really lasts? What even is *real love*? Have we used the word "love" so much that it has now become a second-hand emotion? Do we need a heart when a heart can be broken?

EXPLORING the STATUTES

1 John 4:7-12 – "Dear friends, let us love one another, because love is from God, and everyone who loves has been born of God and knows God. The one who does not love does not know God, because **God is love**. God's love was revealed among us in this way: God sent His One and Only Son into the world so that we might live through Him. Love consists in this: not that we loved God, but that He loved us and sent His Son to be the propitiation for our sins. Dear friends, if God loved us in this way, we also must love one another. No one has ever seen God. If we love one another, God remains in us and His love is perfected in us." (HCSB, emphasis added)

Ephesians 3:17-18 – "I pray that you, being rooted and firmly established in love, may be able to comprehend with all the saints what is the length and width, height and depth of God's love." (HCSB)

Jeremiah 31:3 – "The LORD appeared to him from far away. I have loved you with an everlasting love; therefore, I have continued to extend faithful love to you." (HCSB)

1 Corinthians 13:13- "Now these three remain: faith, hope, and **love**. But the **greatest** of these **is love**." (HCBS)

John 3:16 – "For God loved the world in this way: He gave His One and Only Son, so that everyone who believes in Him will not perish but have eternal life." (HCSB)

Galatians 5:22-28 – "But the fruit of the Spirit is love, joy, peace, patience, kindness, goodness, faith, gentleness, self-control." (HCBS)

Read also – Romans 8:38-39, Psalm 86:5, Lamentations 3:22-26

UNDERSTANDING the SUMMATION

Perhaps in our casual, nonchalant world, we do over-use the word "love." Perhaps in our casual over-use we have unintentionally reduced love to a second-hand emotion. Perhaps, also, because of this over-use, our heart gets broken and trampled and we no longer wish to expose ourselves to the pain. Who needs a heart?

Ironically, on one hand we over use love, and on the other hand we stop using love completely. We create walls to resist intimacy for fear of getting hurt. In the world we live, it's easy to hide behind our computer or phone using the written text instead of face-to-face meetings, thus insolating ourselves from further exposure to love or pain.

However, as Christians we live in God's world, or should I say, Kingdom—not in this casual, nonchalant world of heartbreak and second-hand emotion. I was so inspired and energized after I read the words in 1 John 4:7-12, which tells us that God is love and that His love was revealed when He sent His one and only Son into this world so that we might live through Him. Jesus was brutally beaten, crucified, and died to make a way for us to go to heaven and to free us from an eternity in Hell and cruelty.

Without that single act of "love," no one in this casual, nonchalant world would know the true meaning of love. If we could ask Jesus, "What's love got to do with it or is love a second-hand emotion?" over two thousand years ago, you would have found His answer nailed to a cross. Now, He sits at the right hand of the Father, and His Spirit lives in us.

Who needs a heart, when a heart can be broken? John tells us that we are to love one another. Love is from God, and love is perfected in *us*. We are to use the Spirit that lives within us to love one another. In Galatians, we read about love being one of the fruit of the Spirit. It is a gift from the Holy Spirit. This love perfected in us is God's love that we are called to share with others.

Our heart should break for what breaks God's heart. When we see someone hurting, we are called to reach out and show them God's perfect love. Maybe we are called to share our heartbreak story with them, or maybe we are called to listen. We are always called to use our heart to show God's love to others. God knew our hearts would break, and He knew we would use that heartbreak experience to help others through similar circumstances. Despite the pain and heartbreak, we need our heart to empathize with others and support others through their pain instead of hiding behind walls of fear and regret. Without a heart, none of this compassion for others would be possible. Broken or mended, we all need a heart.

I believe that the greatest act of love we can show others is to fulfill God's great commission by teaching others about Jesus' sacrifice on the cross and leading them down the path to eternal life in heaven. Knowing Jesus is the greatest gift for all of mankind and sharing that gift with others is an honor.

In 1 Corinthians 13:13, Paul, the author, mentions faith, hope, and love. He ends chapter 13 by saying that the greatest of these is love. Paul certainly did not believe that love was a second-hand emotion; quite the opposite. Love is the first in the list of the fruit of the Spirit, and scholars believe that is due to its great importance.

It's logical to conclude that regardless of how we use the term in our everyday lives, love is not a second-hand emotion. God intended love to be of utmost importance and everlasting. God considered the emotion of love as the greatest in a list of many heartfelt emotions.

In Jeremiah God's Word says He will love us with an everlasting love, one that will never end. "Never" and "everlasting" are big words that are somewhat unfathomable for us. There is not much in our society that lasts forever. Everything has an expiration date or a shelf life—everything except for God's love. God's love does not expire; it never ends…never.

The Bible says that God *is* love. Love is not a second-hand emotion; far from it. Love is our God—our everlasting Savior who shed His blood so that we might live forever and our hearts would be mended.

When my oldest son was the director of his college campus ministry called ROOTED, he taught me this Scripture, and I pray this now for you. Ephesians 3:17-18 says, "I pray that the Messiah may dwell in your hearts through faith. I pray that you, being rooted and firmly established in love, may be able to comprehend with all the saints what is the length, width, height and depth of God's love." (HCSB)

God is…my logical conclusion for my Love.
Who is your love?

Notes

Notes

MY HEALER

JOURNEY

Be healed, my child! Have you ever watched any of the TV evangelists lay hands on people and proclaim healing on someone and then they fall to the floor? Pretty unbelievable, right?

I now believe that God can work in all situations to bring glory to His kingdom, but I didn't always. I have also learned not to make fun of something I know nothing about; I had to repent for that one. My story leads me to one of those TV evangelists in my local city.

In the chapter on peace, I briefly mentioned how my world was shattered and my peace was destroyed. If you remember, I described how I went in for a second sonogram after the doctor said the size of the baby appeared small based on the number of weeks pregnant. At that time, I was about nine weeks pregnant when our doctor advised us that there was no longer a heartbeat. I miscarried that baby. Of course, there is more to this story.

That day, as we headed to the doctor's office, it never occurred to my husband and me that we would find no heartbeat. Stories like this just didn't happen to *us*. As the days passed after the sonogram, my thoughts went to blaming myself. I was convinced, or at least was convincing myself, that I must have done something wrong. I must have eaten the wrong food or had a soda or something; I told myself that I would do better next time.

Well, the next time came...and I miscarried again. I couldn't rationalize or process what was happening, nor could I fix it, control it, or stop it. Why was God doing this to us? People were telling us that God must be sparing us from an unhealthy baby. I was hearing all kinds of weird stories about why God was taking the babies to heaven. John and I were confused and defeated and in a dark place. In those days, we were not spiritually or emotionally equipped.

However, that was about to change. My husband was at work during the day. I was home with our two-year-old son and trying to make sense of it all. My journey began with what I now call my "Age of Enlightenment." I began asking questions and yearning to know more about God's character.

I guess deep down I knew that God was good, but I wasn't really sure what that meant for me in this situation. As "fate" would have it (God's fate), I was teaching a women's Bible study called Knowing and Experiencing God. Through this Bible study, I learned through Scriptures that God didn't cause bad things to happen—that was the devil's mission. I had never heard those words before.

I knew what those people were telling me didn't feel right when they made statements like, "God is taking the baby to His flower garden in heaven," or "God is sparing you from life with an unhealthy child." Now, looking back I realize that feeling was the Holy Spirit saying,

"Don't listen to those words. They are not from God." I learned from God's Word that God didn't cause the miscarriages and that I didn't do anything wrong. That knowledge was a paradigm shift. God honored what I knew at the time and brought me through the trial. He then taught me so much more! I have learned over the years that the best learning experiences come while teaching others.

EXPLORING the STATUTES

John 10:10 – "A thief comes only to kill, steal and destroy. I [Jesus] have come so that you may have life and have it in abundance." (HCSB)

John 16:33 – "I have told you these things, so that you may have peace. In this world you will have trouble. But take heart! I have overcome the world." (NIV)

Isaiah 53:5 – "By His wounds we are healed." (NIV) "And with His stripes we are healed." (KJV)

Mark 11:23-24 – "If anyone says to this mountain, 'Be lifted up and thrown into the sea,' and does not doubt in his heart, but believes that what he says will happen, it will be done for him. Therefore, I tell you, all the things you pray and ask for—believe that you have received them, and you will have them." (HCSB)

Read Also: Luke 11: 9-10

UNDERSTANDING the SUMMATION

John 10:10 and John 16:33 are two of my favorite Scriptures still to this day. I had never heard these Scriptures before and they sustained me during this confusing time. Moreover, they fueled me. I began using them to change my belief system and change my frame

of mind.

After the miscarriages, several of my friends and I began searching for more than what we were experiencing. We began attending a Wednesday prayer meeting at a different church, which expanded our spiritual horizons. We learned more and more about God's promises and how to believe and stand on God's Word. In these prayer meetings, I felt like I was getting to know Jesus. Now, when I think back on those days, I smile and sometimes tear up. We had revelation after revelation and so much spiritual growth!

It was that time of my life when I began to make the connection between presenting a case to God and presenting a case to a judge. I grew much closer to God, because I was hungry for His Word and His system of justice. God, the Bible, and prayer became less random and more organized and structured. The Holy Spirit became alive and flowing in my life. I could feel His presence and hear thoughts that could only be coming from God. God's will was becoming less obscure and more focused.

I learned that God didn't *cause* the miscarriages. John 10:10 says that the thief, the devil, comes to kill, steal, and destroy, but Jesus comes to give us life in abundance. I had never heard that Scripture before. Jesus has overcome the world, and by Jesus' wounds I was healed. What was I to do with these Scriptures? I took them to the judge and petitioned for a ruling in my favor. What the devil meant for harm was about to be used for God's glory! This information was about to catapult me into a new level of understanding and power. I was yearning to learn as much as I could about God and His Word. I was hungry for knowledge—biblical knowledge. The spiritual light bulb was growing brighter and brighter.

> I WAS HUNGRY FOR KNOWLEDGE—BIBLICAL KNOWLEDGE.
> THE SPIRITUAL LIGHT BULB WAS GROWING BRIGHTER AND
> BRIGHTER.

One day, in 1998, I went with a friend to a Lindsay Roberts women's conference. (Only God can get a former Catholic onto the campus of Oral Roberts to a women's conference!) I didn't know what to expect. Yes, I was visiting the campus of a TV evangelist about whom I used to make jokes as a kid. This experience was all new for me. I had was a Lutheran at the time, former Catholic, but there I was in the crowd listening to Bible teaching on healing that was beyond anything I had ever known or experienced.

My friend and I were curious to witness faith healings and evangelism. This was definitely the place for such happenings. When Cheryl Salem, Lindsey's sister-in-law, finished speaking, she said, "Someone here is being healed of female issues." I looked at my friend and said, "That's mine; that is for me." We both stood up and went down front for prayer.

Nine months later, my second son was born, and my daughter was born nineteen months following! During those pregnancies, I spoke John 10:10 and John 16:33. I believed that God had healed me that day at the conference. I never once doubted that I would deliver to full term. Jesus overcame the world and brought me life in abundance, just like His Word promised.

God's Word *never* fails. The healing was not for my glory but for His glory and the advancement of God's kingdom. I believe that the miscarriages were not some little distraction; they were part of a bigger plan to destroy God's plan. We think our role in this life is too small. My kids have great significance to God. He has something for them to accomplish, and the devil was (and still is) trying to squash that plan. We all have great significance as parts of God's plan. God is using us to impact the world! But we must first know Jesus and His Word in order to achieve this plan.

I want to share with you the story about the woman in the Bible with the blood issue. In Luke chapter 8, the Bible tells that Jesus was walking from town to town, telling parables, preaching, driving out demons, healing, and raising a child from the dead. I want to focus on verses 43-48. As Jesus was walking and heading to a home to heal a young girl, a woman who had been suffering with a condition for twelve years touched him. The story unfolds as follows:

> A woman in the crowd had suffered for twelve years with constant bleeding, and she could find no cure. Coming up behind Jesus, she touched the fringe of his robe. Immediately, the bleeding stopped. 'Who touched me?' Jesus asked. Everyone denied it, and Peter said, 'Master, this whole crowd is pressing up against you.' But Jesus said, 'Someone deliberately touched me, for I felt healing power go out from me.' When the woman realized that she could not stay hidden, she began to tremble and fell to her knees in front of him. The whole crowd heard her explain why she had touched him and that she had been immediately healed. 'Daughter, he said to her, 'your faith has made you well. Go in peace.'
>
> Luke 8:43-48 (NLT)

I had battled migraine headaches for about fourteen years. These headaches forced me to stop what I was doing and go to bed.

Sometimes I was nauseous. Sometimes they would last for a day—and sometimes they would last for *three* days. Some months I had three headaches, and some months I had twelve headaches. In the beginning, I missed work and kids' events. For fourteen years, I believed for healing and yet continued to suffer with headaches. Eventually, I found very qualified doctors and very innovative medication and treatments. I was not in pain all the time, but I was on medication all the time. I had numerous x-rays, EMGs, MRIs, injections, and even two sinus surgeries. For years, I was standing on the Scriptures; petitioning God for a ruling in my favor.

It's not easy believing God for healing and seeing no results day after day, year after year. It's not easy speaking to the mountain and seeing no movement. Many times, I was happy and faithful on the outside for all to see but in pain and struggling on the inside. I wasn't struggling with my salvation, but I was struggling with why the healing was taking God so long. I wanted this to go away. I spoke to the mountain and believed in my heart and believed I had received the healing. So where was my healing? Where was my Healer? I thanked Him for the healing many times. Standing firm on my belief, I threw the medicine away. Then, when the pain became too unbearable, I refilled the prescription or pulled the medication out of the trash.

I was supposed to be the Christian "rock," the Bible class leader, but I did not see any evidence of this healing. I can and did so easily relate to this woman in the Bible who dealt with her condition for so many years. I would like to talk with her over lunch and hear her story.

Can you picture the scene for the woman with the issue of blood? She probably heard about this man named Jesus walking from town to town, performing miracles. She also probably heard that He had calmed the storm that was raging on the lake or that He drove the demons out of a man and into the pigs. She knew something was different or perhaps special about this man. After twelve years of suffering without finding a cure, this woman saw her opportunity, and she was not going to let it walk on by. This man, Jesus, was coming to her town. Maybe, she thought, she had to speak to Jesus and ask for help. As He walked by, the crowd was so large and so tight that she could only get close enough to touch the fringe on His robe, or the hem on His garment. She grasped for whatever she could get, hoping that she would never have to deal with this suffering again.

I've been there. She must not have been a person of importance in the town, because her name is not mentioned in the Bible. So, I imagine that she didn't want a big scene. However, a big scene is exactly what she got! After she touched Him, can you imagine her surprise? The bleeding stopped; she was healed immediately upon touching the hem of His garment. She had never come face to face with Jesus.

Jesus knew someone touched Him in that moment; someone with a purpose. What made her different from others in the crowd? Peter was puzzled by Jesus' question. Many people that day may have needed healing for any number of ailments. Because of the crowd, they had to have accidently bumped into Jesus, but no power left His body, no healing occurred. However, the woman who purposed to reach out in faith and harness the power of Jesus received her miracle.

That was no accidental bumping into the Healer; it was a deliberate act of faith. You don't *accidently* bump into Jesus and automatically release the healing power. Jesus didn't know who bumped into Him. It's only logical to conclude that He didn't release the healing power; she did with her faith. Thus, it makes sense that *our* faith must release His healing power as well.

HOWEVER, THE WOMAN WHO PURPOSED TO REACH OUT IN FAITH AND HARNESS THE POWER OF JESUS RECEIVED HER MIRACLE. THAT WAS NO ACCIDENTAL BUMPING INTO THE HEALER; IT WAS A DELIBERATE ACT OF FAITH. YOU DON'T ACCI-DENTLY BUMP INTO JESUS AND AUTOMATICALLY RELEASE THE HEALING POWER. JESUS DIDN'T KNOW WHO BUMPED INTO HIM. IT'S ONLY LOGICAL TO CONCLUDE THAT HE DIDN'T RELEASE THE HEALING POWER; SHE DID WITH HER FAITH.

In August of 2015, I was attending a church revival. It was an amazing week of music and speakers. On August 9th, 2015, during the revival, the pastor spoke about someone being healed from a "long standing" condition. When the pastor made the statement that Sunday in August, I felt like the woman with the issue of blood. At first, I was sitting in my seat looking around the church and thinking, "What great news that was for someone." Then, as if a brick hit me, I realized he was talking about *me*. Jesus was walking by.

With every fiber of my being, I purposed to reach out, release my faith to touch Jesus. I said, "Yes, that's me, I am healed!" Jesus must have felt the power leave His body. I haven't had a migraine since! Sure, now the devil tries to come at me with headaches to cause me to doubt, but I believe that my faith healed me that day, just as it did the woman in the Bible. We both could have let Jesus walk on by, but we didn't. We chose to seize the opportunity and extend our faith and release the healing God had for us.

In 2001, after having our third child, my husband and I attended his class reunion. While there, a woman told me that she had one child and was unable to have more children. Her situation haunted me. I couldn't stop thinking about her and how that could have been me.

In 1998 at the Lindsay Roberts conference, I could have let Jesus walk on by. I didn't have to reach out and grab that healing. I could have sat in my seat and let someone else take it. There were over a thousand women in the auditorium. The healing was available to any who had the faith to accept it that day. In August of 2015, I could have let Jesus walk on by. I didn't have to reach out that day either.

What if I had doubted God's ability to heal? What if I had been looking around and not paying attention? What if I just didn't think it was for me?

If that were the case, I would be telling you a different story today...or telling no story at all. I could still be stuck not knowing a Savior who heals or not believing that part of the Bible is real today. If that were the case, I wouldn't have received the healing at the Lindsay Robert's conference, and I would be living without two of my children.

A lack of knowledge keeps us living beneath God's purpose for ourselves and for others. That day, reaching out and touching the fringe on Jesus' robe changed my life. My faith healed me. I know Jesus felt the power leave His body that February day in 1998 and again that August day in 2015. It is my belief that He said, "Daughter, your faith has healed you."

Only God knows the time and place for the healing to best serve His kingdom. I don't know why the woman had the issue of blood for twelve years or why I was attacked with miscarriages and migraine headaches. During those fourteen years, I met Jesus on a deeper level through His Word and Spirit. I also learned to take care of myself with better eating and sleeping habits. I learned more Scriptures than ever before and to pray with more conviction and authority. I know that through both of these trials, I learned to just remain faithful to present the Scriptures to His court and thank Him that His Word will never fail.

Think of how many people over those twelve years knew about the lady with the issue of blood and how the word of her healing must have spread from town to town. What a testimony to be used for God's glory back in her time! And it's still a testimony used to help people today. Giving God the glory and giving people hope is my goal with my story as well.

I don't know what healing you need today. It doesn't matter if you have a cold or an injury or a long-standing illness. I challenge you to call out to God with these Scriptures. Print the Scriptures that are written above and speak them every day. Begin to speak to the mountains in your life. Believe in your heart that they are removed.

Don't just "accidently" bump into Jesus; purpose to use your faith and reach out and draw Him close! Believe that you have received the healing that Jesus gave you according to Isaiah 53:5. Thank God for the healing every day. Stop speaking about the problem, and begin thanking God for your healing. Know that God didn't cause the sickness or injury you are facing.

Don't give up. God hears you. Only God knows when and where the healing will come to give the greatest benefit to His kingdom.

The Scripture says that we are healed by Jesus' stripes, so logically we must conclude that we are healed. Hold on to the knowledge that Jesus has overcome everything in your world and has given you life in abundance.

Don't let Jesus walk on by. Let your faith release the healing power.

I pray that you seize this opportunity to know Jesus and believe for healing and stand firm on Isaiah 53:5. I pray that you speak to whatever mountain needs to be removed and reach out and touch Jesus. He is always nearby waiting for you to extend your faith and release the healing. In Jesus' name, Amen.

God is...my logical conclusion for my Healer.
Who is your healer?

Notes

Notes

MY PROVIDER

JOURNEY

"PROVIDER" is a very unassuming title; this word doesn't seem as biblical and powerful as titles used for my other subjects. As a matter of fact, I have written this word many other times for many other purposes and in many other forms of speech throughout this book.

I have also used the word "provide" often in my legal writing. For example, I might say to someone, "I have been *provided* with the following documents" or ask someone, "Please *provide* copies of all receipts to support your invoices." We have healthcare providers, child-care providers, cell phone-providers, and many other providers. The word "provider" saturates our language. So, why give this word the status as a title to a chapter?

I was married and employed at my first real job both in the same year. As newlyweds, we moved to a town and began our married life together with steady jobs and paychecks for the first time. We were looking for a church to meet both our needs. Tithing wasn't a huge priority, but we were dabbling in it. It was something we thought we were supposed to do. I really had no training in this area other than giving part of whatever was in my wallet at the time. My husband had more of an example set by his parents, but we really were floundering on this issue in our early married life.

Over the next couple of years, we settled on a church and became regular tithing members. What is a regular tithing member of a church? Merriam-Webster's Dictionary defines "tithe" as, "to pay or give a tenth." We began to give a tenth to the church every time we got paid, but only a tenth of our "net" income. We were doing pretty well, financially. Nothing excessive, but our income was comfortable and stable. I guess, in our minds, that "net tenth" was good enough. Less taxes and other company withdrawals, our net income was the money we received to spend, so that was the money we used to tithe.

We didn't understand covenant blessings or the concept of "sowing and reaping." We really didn't know there was a better way. I think that many Christians don't know either. I have to admit, there was a part of me that thought the church just wanted my money. I had no idea that I could or would be blessed in return.

A few years went by, and we moved to a larger town and expanded our spiritual growth. We began to study and learn about Abraham's blessing and God's covenant taught in Genesis 12:1-3. Abraham was to be the father of many nations, and his name would be great. God would bless those who blessed him and curse those who cursed him. We also began learning the spiritual law of planting and harvesting as told in the Parable of the Sower in Matthew 13:3-9, which speaks of planting your seed in good soil and seeking a great harvest. I think the most impactful lesson we learned was the concept found in Malachi 3:8-11. In it, God is telling us to test Him and see if He doesn't open the floodgates of heaven and pour out blessings. This teaching and these Scriptures brought biblical financial concepts into a whole new light for us. My husband and I were ready to change our ways and see what the Lord had to provide.

EXPLORING the STATUTES

Genesis 12:1-3 – "I will make you into a great nation, and I will bless you; I will make your name great, and you will be a blessing. I will bless those who bless you, and whoever curses you I will curse; and all people on earth will be blessed through you." (NIV)

Matthew 13:3-9 – "Once there was a man who went out to sow grain. As he scattered the seed in the field, some of it fell along the path, and the birds came and ate it up. Some of it fell on rocky ground, where there was little soil. The seeds soon sprouted, because the soil wasn't deep. But when the sun came up, it burned the young plants; and because the roots had not grown deep enough, the plants soon dried up. Some of the seed fell among thorn bushes, which grew up and choked the plants. But some seeds fell in good soil, and the plants bore grain: some had one hundred grains, others sixty, and others thirty." (NIV)

Malachi 3:8-11 – "By not making the payments of the tenth and the contributions. You are suffering under a curse, yet you—the whole nation—are still robbing Me. Bring the full tenth into the storehouse so that there may be food in My house. Test Me in this way,' says the LORD of Hosts. 'See if I will not open the floodgates of heaven and pour out a blessing for you without measure. I will rebuke the devourer for you, so that it will not ruin the produce of your land and your vine in your field will not fail to produce fruit,' says the LORD of Hosts." (HCSB)

Luke 6:38 – "Give and it shall be given unto you. A good measure, pressed down, shaken together and running over, will be poured into your lap. For with the measure you use, it will be measured to you." (HCSB)

James 1:22 – "Be a doer of the Word, and not hearers only, deceiving yourselves." (HCSB)

Philippians 4:19 – "And my God will supply all your needs according to His riches in glory in Christ Jesus." (HCSB)

See also: Psalm 84:11, Matthew 25:14 Parable of three servants and the talents, Hebrews 13:5, Deuteronomy 8:18 and 2 Corinthians 9:6-11.

UNDERSTANDING the SUMMATION

My husband and I finally decided that we no longer wanted "net" blessings; we wanted more. You see, all along God was "providing" the means for us to obtain greater blessings, but we were not meeting our end of the bargain. If we were in a contract with God, we were not fulfilling our end of the contract. In effect, by not tithing on our full gross income, we had *tied God's hands*. In legal terms, He was not obligated to fulfill His end of the contract because we were in breach of contract.

According to Malachi 3:10, we were robbing God by not paying the full tenth; therefore, we were suffering under a curse. The floodgates of heaven could not open and blessings could flow upon us. Moreover, God could not rebuke the devourer on our behalf. Also, in Luke 6:38, it says we are to give and it will be given to you and that in the same measure you give, it will be measured back to you. OH, HELLO!

God was "providing" the means for blessings to be poured upon us, but we were providing a weak measuring stick. If we don't give, nothing can be given back to us. When we give a little, then a little will be given back to us. By giving on our net income, only net blessing could be given back—or possibly nothing at all. Net giving is not really tithing at all. In order to untie God's hands, we have to be *doers* of God's Word.

Consequently, we changed our ways and began tithing on our *entire* income. The tithe check is the first check we write. We want to give our first fruit to the Lord. We learned that Abraham's blessing passes down to us, not just for our benefit but for us to use to *bless others*. God will bless those who bless us and curse those who curse us. Through our obedience, we met our contractual obligation, which allowed God to fulfill His promise to us.

> THROUGH OUR OBEDIENCE, WE MET OUR CONTRACTUAL OBLIGATION, WHICH ALLOWED GOD TO FULFILL HIS PROMISE TO US. NOW, HIS BLESSINGS ABOUND TO US AND FLOW THROUGH US.

Now, His blessings abound to us and flow through us to others. Not only has God somehow turned on my radar for those around me who could use help, but He has "provided" new avenues for me to gain favor as I seek others to join in my philanthropic efforts on His behalf. Providing for others in need is one of our family's most rewarding joys in life.

I want to touch on the principle of planting and harvesting, also called sowing and reaping, briefly. When I was out of work for those months, I had the best time due in large part to seeds planted earlier in the year. I believe that I had such Godly friends around me while I was not working because I cultivated friendships in a small group from church. Earlier in the summer, I was obedient to God's nudging, and I attended the small group training session at my church. I began leading a small group a month before my work situation changed. These beautiful friendships sustained me during my time at home when I felt alone.

Good seed planted for a later harvest is a basic fundamental kingdom principle. God says, give and it shall be given to you with the same measure that you give. "The plans of the diligent lead surely to abundance and advantage, but everyone who acts in haste comes surely to poverty" (Proverbs 21:5 AMP). This seed and harvest principle just makes sense.

My husband and I purposed to plant a good seed and tithe into good soil. We tithe to a good Bible-based church that in turn gives to other worthy missions who support God's work around the world. We support local charities that do God's work in our community. We believe part of planting seed into good soil is also contributing to the lives of our kids and others.

It is important to plant good seed in our marriage, children, friendships, and career if we expect to harvest quality and excellence in those areas. In other words, be a good spouse to get a good spouse; be a good parent to get good kids; be a good friend to get a good friend; and be a good employer to get good employees; or be a good employee to get advancement. You have to invest into improving the very idea that you crave to see improvement. You don't reap the reward without diligently seeking the harvest.

If you are praying and believing for some new event or happening right now, write down your vision, be obedient to God, and then diligently work towards that goal. Plant seeds into your dream. If you want a new car, while you're working to save money, wash cars and care for someone else's car. If you want to get married, always present yourself as a worthy, godly mate for someone. If you want a baby, keep yourself healthy and throw a baby shower or babysit for your friends. Good life lessons come while we wait, *patiently*, on the Lord. Sometimes, the journey is painful, but God's reward is always worth the wait.

When times get tough, and they as always do, my husband and I stand on God's Word. We take God's statutes to His High Court and remind Him of His promises. In Malachi 3:10, God says *test* Him. We remind God that His Word says if we bring the entire tenth into the store house, He will open the floodgates of heaven and pour out blessings without measure, and we expect Him to rebuke the devourer. We thank Him for His Word and we expect the blessings without measure.

While I was not working for so many months, I was blessed to have great friends and this book to write. I also was blessed with a wonderful spiritual awakening that would not have happened without the time away from the office. Blessings can come in many forms. Money doesn't just fall from the sky. God provides what we need when we need it. God provides ideas for extra income. He provides good health. He provides divine meetings for business deals. He provides favor and acceptance in certain situations to propel us forward. He provides strong friendships and strong marriages.

I don't think these ideas and situations are accidental; it is logical to conclude that all of this provision is the opening of heaven's floodgates and the pouring out of blessing without measure. God supplies all of our needs according to His riches and glory, not according to the world's riches and glory. AMEN!

Why did I use the unassuming word "Provider" as a title to a chapter? It's simple really—because God is my financial Provider, my healthcare Provider, my childcare Provider, but mostly, my spiritual

Provider. When I am obedient and plant godly seeds and tithe and put Him first, God is faithful to provide all.

I pray that you will be a doer of the Word and untie God's hands. Allow God to "provide" for you. Bring your tenth into the storehouse so that God will open the floodgates of heaven, rebuke the devourer, and pour out blessings without measure upon your life. I pray that you allow those blessings to flow through you to those in your world who need help. I also pray that God will supply all of your needs according to His riches and glory, in Christ Jesus. In His name, Amen.

God is...my logical conclusion for my Provider.
Who is your provider?

Notes

Notes

MY PERFECTION

JOURNEY

"If I were a super hero, I would want the super power of never making a mistake!" I said from the driver's seat. "That's so lame", was the response I received from my youngest son and his friend, who were sitting in the back seats. They went on to say there are so many better super powers to have and, as you can imagine with teenage boys, a detailed discussion transpired about super powers.

I interrupted to tell them that I was mainly frustrated about frequently hitting the send button on group emails and later discovering typos. This was after I spell checked and proofread the email, but in my haste, I always seemed to miss something! I could never get the email perfect. They still were not impressed with the power. So, I asked them to consider never making a mistake at anything, anytime—on homework or on a test, or in a game or talking with a girl.

"Could you imagine *never* making a mistake?" They were beginning to grasp the bigger picture. I caught myself pondering the bigger picture as well.

When I was younger, I really didn't like dishes to sit in the sink or laundry to sit in the dryer overnight. I preferred that all items be placed, nice and tidy, in their spots. I wanted my house and my "stuff" to look *perfect*. Neatness wasn't just preferred, it was expected. I felt the same way about my car, my hair, and my nails. I always wanted to say the right thing and do the right thing. It was quite exhausting trying to keep things perfect and trying not to mess something up.

Then I had a family. Of course, I wanted them to be perfect, too. So, I pushed my desires on them.

I am blessed with a wonderful husband. He is an exceptional father. He helps around the house and provides a great living for our family. My kids are great kids and excel in all aspects of life. I wanted life to float along smoothly and easy. I wanted my family to be perfect—their grades, their rooms, and even their friends.

I thought that's what everyone was striving to achieve…the perfect life. I thought if we did everything "right," nothing would go "wrong."

Sure, I worried about all the "what if's" that might happen along the way that could go wrong to destroy my perfect life. My goal was to control all of the "what ifs." While the kids were young, perfection and control was easier, but as they grew up, I realized I couldn't control life. I learned that my idea of perfection was not the same as the people in the rest of the world, especially the people in my own house.

At work, making a mistake is unspeakable for me. Does anyone want that phone call? You know, the one that advises you of the error in your calculations or the typo on your report to the executive team? I really don't even want to be corrected by my best employee that I hired because I knew she would be a great asset to my team. Correction is for other people, not me. In my mind, mistakes are just something most of us try to avoid.

Is perfection the goal we are all seeking?

EXPLORING the STATUTES

In the book of Luke we read about the different approach taken by Mary and Martha when Jesus visited their house.

Luke 10:38- 42 –

As Jesus and his disciples were on their way, he came to a village where a woman named Martha opened her home to him. She had a sister called Mary, who sat at the Lord's feet listening to what he said. But Martha was distracted by all the preparations that had to be made. She came to him and asked, 'Lord, don't you care that my sister has left me to do the work by myself? Tell her to help me!'

'Martha, Martha,' the Lord answered, 'you are worried and upset about many things, but few things are needed—or indeed only one. Mary has chosen what is better, and it will not be taken away from her.'

(NIV)

2 Corinthians 12:9 – "My grace is sufficient for you, for my power is made perfect in weakness." Paul said, "Therefore, I will boast all the more gladly about my weaknesses, so that Christ's power may rest on me. That is why for Christ's sake, I delight in weaknesses, in insults, in hardships, in persecutions in difficulties. For when I am weak, then I am strong." (NIV)

Genesis 1:27 – "So, God created mankind in His own image." (NIV)

Galatians 1:10 – "Am I now trying to win the approval of human beings or of God? Or am I trying to please people? If I were still trying to please people, I would not be a servant of Christ." (NIV)

Proverbs 21:5 – "The plans of the diligent lead to profit." (NIV)

1 Peter 2:22 – "He did not commit a sin, and no deceit was found in His mouth." (HCSB)

2 Corinthians 5:20-21 – "Therefore, we are ambassadors for Christ, as though God were making an appeal through us; we beg you on behalf of Christ, be reconciled to God. He made Him who knew no sin to be sin on our behalf, so that we might become the righteousness of God in Him." (NASB)

UNDERSTANDING the SUMMATION

Why was Martha concerned with tasks when Jesus came to her house? Why was she working so hard with all of the preparations? She was about to have company—but not just any company. The Messiah was coming to her house for dinner and bringing His friends! I believe that she working so hard because she wanted everything perfect. Only after everything was in its place would she sit down and enjoy His company. Like I did, she wanted everyone in her house to think like her, especially Mary.

But in her effort to achieve perfection in her surroundings, Martha was missing what she needed most—Jesus, sitting right in front of her.

In Galatians 1:10, the Bible asks us if we are trying to win the approval of people...or win the approval of God. Whose approval was

Martha seeking that day? Whose approval are any of us seeking when we are striving for perfection?

In 2 Corinthians 5:21-22, we learn that Jesus knew no sin so that we could be made righteous in Him. We should not be striving for perfection; we have been made the righteousness in Christ Jesus. Righteousness cannot be earned; it was given.

The Bible says we were created in God's image. We already look like Him and have the ability to work and achieve according to His plan. The Bible says in Proverbs 21:5 that our diligence leads to abundance and advantage.

Based on these statutes, it is logical to believe that we should be striving—not for perfection, but for *excellence*. We should be diligently working to achieve what God has placed in our lives. Excellence can be achieved through hard work and persistence, not through the fear of something going wrong. When we work hard and show that we are good stewards, then God bestows blessings of abundance and advantage upon us. When we are constantly striving to reach perfection, we will always fall short and we will miss the good things that are happening right in front of us.

> IN 2 CORINTHIANS 5:21-22, WE LEARN THAT JESUS KNEW NO SIN SO THAT WE COULD BE MADE RIGHTEOUS IN HIM. WE SHOULD NOT BE STRIVING FOR PERFECTION; WE HAVE BEEN MADE THE RIGHTEOUSNESS IN CHRIST JESUS. RIGHTEOUSNESS CANNOT BE EARNED; IT WAS GIVEN. THE BIBLE SAYS WE WERE CREATED IN GOD'S IMAGE. WE ALREADY LOOK LIKE HIM AND HAVE THE ABILITY TO WORK AND ACHIEVE ACCORDING TO HIS PLAN.

Here's the thing: I can relate to Martha. I want things perfect and want others to help me in my efforts. But no matter how hard I try, I am not perfect. My husband isn't perfect. My kids aren't perfect. My work isn't perfect. My house sure isn't perfect. My writing isn't perfect. Nothing in my life has ever been perfect, because I have never been nor ever will be perfect.

Just like Martha, I can busy myself as much as possible, searching for approval in the wrong places, but I will never achieve perfection through my own efforts.

And, that's okay.

The Bible says that God's grace is sufficient for me, and His power is made *perfect* in my weakness. In 2 Corinthians 12:9, Paul said that he would delight in his weakness and in his hardships. For when I am weak, then I am strong, because it is in my weakest moments that God's power really shines brightest through me.

Our perfection does not make us right with God, nor does our imperfection condemn us. We have been made righteous through Christ. It is through the death of Jesus Christ on the cross and His resurrection that we are reconciled and made right with God, not through any acts of perfection we strive to achieve.

Don't get me wrong, we shouldn't give up on doing things well and with excellence. I believe that we should always use our talents to their fullest and seek God's glory. It's logical that we should give our best effort to achieve excellence in all that we endeavor. But it's time to take a lesson from Mary and spend less time seeking perfection and more time sitting at the feet of Jesus.

My prayer is that you get off the "perfection" merry-go-round and become a God pleaser, not a people pleaser. I pray that in your

Christian walk you begin to strive for excellence, not perfection, and that God's power will be made perfect in your weakness.

God is…my logical conclusion for my Perfection
(but only in my weakness am I made perfect).
Who are you seeking for perfection?

Notes

MY PROTECTION

JOURNEY

I used to label myself the Co-Head of the household. My father-in-law used to call the house and ask to speak to the head of the household. My response was, "You're speaking to the Co-Head of the household." He would kind of growl under his breath and rather abruptly command me to give the phone to his son. I would just giggle and hand the phone to my husband.

However, over the years, my statement became no laughing matter. I was doing myself a huge disservice and, unknowingly, cursing myself and my marriage. What was I thinking?

Early in our marriage, I was misguided in my understanding of my role as a wife, and it took its toll. I grew up in a generation when men were very dominant and chauvinistic. A woman's place was thought to be in the kitchen. My father was a good man, but very assertive. My father-in-law had doubts about me attending and completing law school. He was ornery, so was I. I proved him wrong and completed law school. Fortunately, my husband did not share these views and supported my law endeavors.

Bear with me while I demonstrate for you how this story and several others all relate to protection. Speeding down the highway doesn't seem like such a big deal. We all push the speed limit at least five mph over. Is that okay? What about failing to report a cash deal on our income tax form to avoid paying the IRS? Is that okay? Everybody does these things. Everybody watches the wrong kind of TV shows or movies sometimes and tells or listens to questionable jokes occasionally. We all gossip and look at people of the opposite sex maybe a little longer than we should. A little bit of this stuff is okay, right?

Or is it? We know not to steal or murder—the really wrong, big ticket items—but what about the marginal acts or the acts that no one will ever know? Where is the line? Do we rely on society to draw our line? Or does God's Word draw our line?

One spring morning, I was driving to my son's jazz band performance. The drive would take me an hour and a half, and I was running late for a performance that would last only about five minutes. It was just me and the highway; no humanity for miles. My cruise control was set to the speed limit. My favorite preacher on my iPhone podcast stopped working. I looked down for a second to restart the podcast. When my eyes returned to the road, a deer was travelling in the grass alongside me. From the deer's perspective, there was a beautiful, green field to the right and a highway to the left. Not knowing which the deer was going to choose, I hit the brakes and slowed. Instead of running into the field, the deer turned left and crossed in front of my path, narrowly missing my car. The deer then leaped the metal center median and ran into the field on the left side of the highway.

Another time while driving home from work, I was once again in a hurry, and this time I was behind the slowest driver on a single-lane road. I couldn't get around her until we reached the intersection where the lanes split and I could pull up beside her. I was sitting at the stop light to her right waiting for the light to change, fully intending to beat her off the line and pass her before the lane narrowed back to single. A note in my cup holder caught my attention and I looked down and began to read the paper. While I was not paying attention, the light turned green and the slower car pulled ahead of me into the intersection. Looking up from the cup holder, I was somewhat frustrated with myself at my lack of focus on my starting line task. However, out of the corner of my right eye, I saw an older truck barreling out of control and heading right for the slower car. The truck T-boned her and continued until finally coming to a stop down the road. The brakes had failed on the truck and the driver couldn't stop. Everyone was fine, but both vehicles were quite damaged, and the woman in the slow car was shaken-up. I was unharmed.

For months, I was out of work during an industry-wide slump in the oil business. Half of our income was suddenly gone. Financially, times were tough at our house. We were cutting back in all areas of our lives. It was a lean time, and we had to turn down many invitations to a lot of fun events. We tightened our financial belt all the way to the tightest notch. The enemy continually filled our minds with doubt and fear about the future. I daily heard thoughts that if we wouldn't tithe, we would have extra money to enjoy all those fun plans. I sent out resumes and looked to broaden my realm of potential employment opportunities. It appeared to us that my situation was stagnant. However, we chose to focus on God's Word. We knew those thoughts were lies. We knew we had to remain faithful to His Word and God would destroy the devourer on our behalf. We never missed our tithe and we donated to the college campus ministry that our son was

leading at the time. We even donated in our local community in both time and money.

So why are these stories important? I'll tell you shortly.

EXPLORING the STATUTES

Psalm 91

Whoever dwells in the shelter of the Most High will rest in the shadow of the Almighty. I will say of the LORD, 'He is my refuge and my fortress, my God, in whom I trust.' Surely he will save you from the fowler's snare and from the deadly pestilence. He will cover you with his feathers, and under his wings you will find refuge; his faithfulness will be your shield and rampart. You will not fear the terror of night, nor the arrow that flies by day, nor the pestilence that stalks in the darkness, nor the plague that destroys at midday. A thousand may fall at your side, ten thousand at your right hand, but it will not come near you. You will only observe with your eyes and see the punishment of the wicked. If you say, 'The LORD is my refuge,' and you make the Most High your dwelling, no harm will overtake you, no disaster will come near your tent. For he will command his angels concerning you to guard you in all your ways; they will lift you up in their hands, so that you will not strike your foot against a stone. You will tread on the lion and the cobra; you will trample the great lion and the serpent. 'Because he loves me,' says the LORD, 'I will rescue him; I will protect him, for he acknowledges my name. He will call on me, and I will answer him; I will be with him in trouble, I will deliver him and honor him. With long life I will satisfy him and show him my salvation.' (NIV)

Define "Dwell" – To remain for a time; to keep the attention directed (Merriam-Webster.com Dictionary)

Ephesians 5:22, 23 – "Wives, submit to your own husbands as to the Lord, for the husband is the head of the wife as Christ is the head of the church." (HCSB)

Isaiah 54:17 – "No **weapon** formed against you will succeed, and you will refute any accusation raised against you in court. This is the heritage of the Lord's servants, and their righteousness is from Me." This is the Lord's declaration." (HCSB emphasis added)

Ephesians 6:11-13 – "Put on the full armor of God so that you can stand against the tactics of the Devil. For our battle is not against flesh and blood, but against the rulers, against the authorities, against the world powers of this darkness, against the spiritual forces of evil in the heavens. This is why you must take up the full armor of God, so that you may be able to resist in the evil day, and having prepared everything, to take your stand." HCSB

Malachi 3:8-11 – "'By not making the payments of the tenth and the contributions, You are suffering under a curse, yet you—the whole nation—are still robbing Me. Bring the full tenth into the storehouse so that there may be food in My house. Test Me in this way,' says the LORD of Hosts. 'See if I will not open the floodgates of heaven and pour out a blessing for you without measure. I will **rebuke the devourer for you**, so that it will not ruin the produce of your land and your vine in your field will not fail to produce fruit,'" says the LORD of Hosts. (HCSB emphasis added)

Define "Rebuke" – to turn back or keep down

Also Read: Psalm 9:10, Job 1:9

UNDERSTANDING the SUMMATION

Why are all of the stories I told you earlier relevant to a discussion on God's protection? They are important because they demonstrate how obedience to God's Word fortifies the shields of God's hedge of protection.

We have to submit to God's Word. What protection would God provide if I was claiming the role as head of the house over my husband? What protection would God provide if I continued to tithe on our net income or abandoned the tithe all together? Speeding and gossiping and those other lesser, "marginal" sins all have one thing in common—they are acts of disobedience to God. When we live a lifestyle filled with these actions, we aren't dwelling in the shelter of the Most High, and our protection lifts. However, we serve a loving God who is kind and merciful when we fall short just as we are with our own kids. Jesus picks us up, and His Word helps us get back on the path to serving Him. Psalm 91 shows us that we receive protection from the Lord when we dwell in him. We must keep our attention on Him. Defiance and disobedience are not actions that contribute to dwelling in Him; therefore, they lift our protective shield.

Similarly, in Malachi 3:10 we learn exactly what steps to take for God to open the floodgates of heaven and also for God to rebuke the devourer. In legal terms, if we don't perform our contractual obligations and bring our full tithe to God, we are in breach of contract. God is no longer bound to fulfill His contractual obligations, and we suffer under a curse. God says, "Test me in this way." He wants us to try it. Start tithing and determine for yourself if the floodgates open and pour out blessings without measure. Test and see if the devourer is rebuked and turned away on your behalf.

If we follow God's commands, we are protected in our marriages, on the roadways, and in our finances, in our health and all areas of life. I can only imagine the definition of "blessings without measure", but I am sure God's definition is far more impressive than anything I can create.

Wives, submit to your husbands. "God, you have GOT to be kidding me!" Yes, I spoke those words, along with, "God must NOT be talking about this day and age." In the early years of my marriage, I maintained my status as the Co-Head of the household. My husband and I both had advanced degrees, and we earned about the same income. I couldn't understand why God would ask me to submit to my husband. There was nothing about that Scripture that I could embrace. So, I just ignored it.

Psalm 91 reads that whoever dwells in the shelter of the Most High will rest in the shelter of the Almighty. The psalmist also wrote that we will find refuge under His wings, no disaster will come near our tent, and He will command His angels to guard us. One definition of "dwell" found in Merriam-Webster.com is to keep the attention directed.

Here's the drawback to my actions. When I ignored God's command to submit to my husband, I made a conscious decision to keep my attention directed away from God. I was dwelling outside the shelter of the Most High and therefore outside of His shadow of protection. All of the Psalm 91 protection was unavailable to me. My own actions had tied God's hands and prevented His protective covering. Furthermore, I was leading a women's Bible study, and John and I were leading our church's high school youth group. For a time, we were not setting a godly example in our own home.

As I mentioned in chapter six, during the early part of our marriage, John and I did not bring the whole tithe into the storehouse.

We were only tithing on our net income, not our gross income. We were robbing God of His money and suffering under a curse. Instead of blessings without measure, we were living under a curse. There was no protection from the devourer. God wasn't free to open the floodgates of Heaven and pour out upon us.

So, in the early years, how were we getting by? First, we didn't know these Scriptures. That's no excuse, and we were floundering a bit. Second, we were unsatisfied with our jobs. We were not growing spiritually or financially. I would say we were just meandering down life's road aimlessly with no clear direction. We had changed our lifestyle some, but we were not sold out or on fire for the Lord. We would probably have been considered somewhere in the lukewarm category…until Satan made a huge mistake.

He hit us too hard when he threw the miscarriages at us. When that fiery dart came our way, we were not equipped spiritually. During that trial, we were faced with a spiritual fork in the road; give up and accept our current situation or take the path of greater knowledge and deeper commitment to God's word. Giving up was not an option. We chose to shed the lukewarm lifestyle and jump into the deeper, hotter water.

I have already mentioned in an earlier chapter that it was my "Age of Enlightenment." For the first time in my life, when I read Ephesians 5:22-23, my eyes were opened. God was asking me to submit to my own husband, *as to the Lord*, for the husband is the head of the wife as Christ is the head of the Church. I had never seen the last part of these verses. It was as if my eyes had been blinded to the words, "as to the Lord." I truly had never noticed them before, and now they magically appeared.

I do now submit to my husband, freely and willingly. The struggle was in my mind, not John's. He was patient with me as I worked through the process. My husband was designed by God to be the head, and he is so much more qualified for the job. It's not that I expected John to be some oppressive ruler, but I was deceived into believing that I was equally (or better) qualified for that particular job. Once I began to truly seek God's heart, His Word became alive in me. God revealed to me that my role as John's wife was of equal importance—as important as the church is to Christ. The job of wife is my place to excel. With God first and both John and I in our rightful roles, our marriage grew stronger than ever before.

John and I had the same experience with Malachi 3:8-11. God's Word began to convict us to tithe on our gross income. If God is going to promise to open the floodgates of heaven and pour out blessings without measure, then I want to do my part to make sure that happens! If God is going to rebuke the devourer for me, then I want to follow God's step-by-step instructions to insure that outcome.

During the downturn in the economy, when I was out of work, we never missed our tithe. We stood on Malachi 3:8-10. We believed that God would see His Word to completion. We knew that blessings would pour out from heaven and He would rebuke the devourer. Rebuke defined, is to turn back or keep down. His Word does not fail. We knew that our family and home would be protected, and it was. The devourer was kept down and turned away. God began providing other sources of income and blessings. I began writing this book.

Our children respect and honor us; that's a blessing without measure. We are healthy. We have great friends. God was keeping His promise. God knew the economy was going to fail, and it will fail again. But we live in God's economy. If we had spent our tithe on fun

> WE BELIEVED THAT GOD WOULD SEE HIS WORD TO COMPLE-
> TION. WE KNEW THAT BLESSINGS WOULD POUR OUT FROM
> HEAVEN AND HE WOULD REBUKE THE DEVOURER. REBUKE
> DEFINED, IS TO TURN BACK OR KEEP DOWN. HIS WORD DOES
> NOT FAIL. WE KNEW THAT OUR FAMILY AND HOME WOULD
> BE PROTECTED, AND IT WAS. THE DEVOURER WAS KEPT DOWN
> AND TURNED AWAY.

activities or clothes and dinner out with friends, what do you think would have happened to our financial security? I believe the devourer would have turned toward us, not away. That is a terrifying thought. Instead, we have been blessed without measure over and over again. Once we let go of our hold on God's money, our lives changed forever.

There is no doubt in my mind that those days I was driving and obeying the speed limit, God was protecting me from the deer and from the driver without brakes. I was hidden under God's wings. I don't know what would have happened if I had been speeding those days or any other day. When I do speed, I get caught and ticketed. That is *not* a blessing. High income taxes are *not* a blessing either. I am self-employed and pay a great deal of income tax, always by the book. What *is* a blessing is that a high tax debt equates to a high work load, and God always provides both the work and the money for tax burden.

It is logical to believe that when we dwell in Him and remain under God's umbrella of protection, we allow God to hide us under His wings and send His angels to guard us and satisfy us with long life. He says no disaster will come near our tent, and He will rebuke the devourer for us. Under His wings is where I want to live, with angels surrounding me and protecting me from the devourer.

During my "Age of Enlightenment," I moved inside the shelter of the Almighty. My focus turned to God, His Scriptures, and pleasing Him. You could say that I began to "dwell" in the shadow of the Most High. The Holy Spirit has prompted me to no longer *want* to speed or watch inappropriate shows or partake in inappropriate conversations. Now I find that I don't want to be a part of gossip and discord. My lifestyle changed from one of self-focus to one of God-focus. My attention is now directed to Him and His kingdom, not mine. I am finally dwelling in the shadow of the Most High.

Because I dwell in Him, I can go to God and seek all of the protection provided in Psalm 91. As a matter of fact, I try to pray Psalm 91 protection every day. I insert my family's name in wherever appropriate instead of the pre-printed pronouns. I also pray Isaiah 54:17; when someone is trying to speak against my family, I pray, "No **weapon** formed against the Moriarty family will succeed, and I refute any accusation raised against us in God's court." I pray that my family has on the full armor of God and we take our stand against the devil's tactics (see Ephesians 6:11-13). I pray these prayers over my husband, who travels, my teenage drivers, my kids' well being, my extended family, my small group ladies, and my property. I stand firm and believe on these protection Scriptures.

Keep in mind that we live in a fallen world where bad things sometimes happen to good people for no apparent reason. That is when the Holy Spirit becomes our comforter and guide. It is so important to stay connected to Him and abide in Him. However, some of this protection is just simply common sense and not a magic formula. For example, someone who continually drives at very high speed is more likely to get injured in an accident than someone who drives at a slower speed.

Someone with heart disease shouldn't expect God's protection from a heart attack while eating French fries and drinking milk shakes every day. On the other hand, I believe protection is orchestrated by God as a result of a lifestyle of obedience to Him. In my two driving situations mentioned above, God protected me from the deer and from the driver with failing brakes due to my regular driving obedience. God also protected my family during the downturn in the economy because of my obedience to tithe on a regular basis.

We are human, which means daily we fall short and make mistakes. There are times when I catch myself speeding or gossiping or doing something that isn't so godly. None of us is perfect; our flesh has desires that are sometimes difficult to keep under control. The devil is good at throwing every temptation at us until we succumb to something we shouldn't. That is normal. I don't believe God protects us when we are good and removes His protection when we make mistakes. I believe that as long as we maintain a *lifestyle* seeking Him, the protection offered in Psalm 91 is available to us. If I miss a day of asking for protection for my family, God isn't going to take that protection away. If I speed or gossip on occasion, God isn't going to turn off the protection button. That is not the God we serve.

We should be striving to be better today than yesterday and better tomorrow than today. In 2 Corinthians 12:9, Paul says that God's grace is sufficient and His power is made perfect in our weakness. The more we seek Him and seek to know Him, following His commands will become easier and remaining under his hedge of protection will be second nature to us. We aren't alone in this endeavor. His spirit in us will prompt us and lead us toward a more Godly and Holy lifestyle.

The Holy Spirit will help us turn away from those temptations that come our way, and when we stumble, Jesus will forgive us for our times of weakness. His grace and mercy are sufficient to comfort us when we fall. We should purpose to keep our attention directed on Jesus and not on whether we fall short. Our protection comes from serving Him, not from achieving a higher level of goodness. I pray that you put on your armor and take your stand against the devil's tactics. I pray that you spend your life dwelling in the shadow of the Most High and abiding by His commands, thus opening the door to God's protection and allowing God's blessings to pour out from heaven without measure. Amen!

God is...my logical conclusion for my Protection.
Who are you seeking for protection?

Notes

9

MY FORGIVENESS

JOURNEY

"I forgive you," or, "I am sorry"—which would you rather say, and which would you rather hear? I would presume you would rather hear "I am sorry" and say "I forgive you." There is emotion behind both of them. It's a long and winding road. The road to forgiveness is not always straight or short; sometimes it's quite long, bumpy, and curvy. Sometimes, forgiveness is the road less traveled, as we choose the path of unforgiveness. I have traveled both many times with great humility and heartbreak.

We can view forgiveness in several categories: the need to forgive others, the need to forgive ourselves, the need to be forgiven by others, and the need to be forgiven by God.

I have been hurt, deeply hurt, a few times in my life. Sure, I have been angry over little things many times, but those little things disappear. I think we could all agree that the little things have no impact on our ability to trust or love. It's the big ticket items that punch us in the face and stick with us to change our perspective forever. Those are the deep hurts to which I am referring.

While in college, I was in love with a guy who wanted to date me while at the same time dating others. I was not about to share. His actions deeply hurt me. This sounds petty and insignificant, but I was crushed, and I spent my college years carrying this pain. I went through a mourning process that lasted for years.

I was sure that I hated the guy and would never forgive him. I tried to move past the heartbreak, but later I learned that the break-up was the best thing for me. Four long years later, I began dating this same guy and later married him. However, without traveling down the road of forgiveness, I would have missed a great man and a great marriage.

> HOWEVER, WITHOUT TRAVELING DOWN THE ROAD OF FORGIVENESS, I WOULD HAVE MISSED A GREAT MAN AND A GREAT MARRIAGE.

Several years ago, someone that we assumed was trustworthy stole a priceless heirloom from our family home. My mother's wedding ring was sold to a pawnshop and lost forever. My Father has been deceased for many years, and there is no way to replace the ring given on their wedding day. I was planning to pass this ring to my daughter. I am the only daughter, and she is the only granddaughter. It made me angry and hurt and frustrated for a very long time. The only way to put this event behind me is to forgive the person, which is not such an easy task.

Most of my apologies have come as a result of my mouth. I talk a lot. My brothers called me "Mouth" when I was growing up. Little did they know they were proclaiming upon me a life-long personality trait. As an adult, I have taken personality tests, and some of the tests predict where you should serve in the Body of Christ. Of course, the tests even proclaimed me as the "Mouth" of the Body of Christ. My mouth has gotten me in trouble so many times! I can't tell you how many phone calls I have made over the years, apologizing for something I said, usually unintentionally. I have also had to apologize to my husband and kids and other family members for statements I made out of anger and frustration.

How many times do we know the right action, but do the wrong thing? We want to please God, but our flesh takes over. We speed down the highway, we curse, we get angry and lash-out, we over-eat, we judge others, and we gossip. We do the things we shouldn't and don't do the things we should. We plan to help others or spend more time with God, and then we get too busy with something else. Maybe we have made mistakes that have hurt others. All these shortfalls cause us to look inward and see our weaknesses and failures, but how we handle them is incredibly important to our future well-being.

When you stumble and fall—and we all fall—do you beat yourself up, or do you pick yourself up? Do you work through a process and forgive yourself, or do you wallow in self-pity? The key to forgiving ourselves is found in recognizing our forgiveness from God.

EXPLORING the STATUTES

John 20:21-23 – "'Again Jesus said, "Peace be with you! As the Father has sent me, I am sending you.' And with that he breathed on them and said, 'Receive the Holy Spirit. If you forgive anyone's sins, their sins are forgiven; if you do not forgive them, they are not forgiven.'" (NIV)

MY LOGICAL CONCLUSION

Colossians 3:12-13 – "Therefore, God's chosen ones, holy and loved, put on heartfelt compassion, kindness, humility, gentleness, and patience, accepting one another and forgiving one another if anyone has a complaint against another. Just as the Lord has forgiven you, so you must also forgive." (HCSB)

Matthew 18:21-35 tells us the story of a slave who would not forgive when he had been forgiven.

> Then Peter came to Him and said, "Lord, how many times could my brother sin against me and I forgive him? As many as seven times?" "I tell you, not as many as seven," Jesus said to him, "but 70 times seven. For this reason, the kingdom of heaven can be compared to a king who wanted to settle accounts with his slaves. When he began to settle accounts, one who owed 10,000 talents was brought before him. Since he had no way to pay it back, his master commanded that he, his wife, his children, and everything he had be sold to pay the debt.
>
> "At this, the slave fell facedown before him and said, 'Be patient with me, and I will pay you everything!' Then the master of that slave had compassion, released him, and forgave him the loan.
>
> "But that slave went out and found one of his fellow slaves who owed him 100 denarii. He grabbed him, started choking him, and said, 'Pay what you owe!'
>
> "At this, his fellow slave fell down and began begging him, 'Be patient with me, and I will pay you back.' But he wasn't willing. On the contrary, he went and threw him into prison until he could pay what was owed. When the other slaves saw what had taken place, they were deeply distressed and went and reported to their master everything that had happened.
>
> "Then, after he had summoned him, his master said to him, 'You wicked slave! I forgave you all that debt because you begged me. Shouldn't you also have had mercy on your fellow slave, as I had mercy on you?' And

86

*his master got angry and handed him over to the jailers to be tortured
until he could pay everything that was owed. So My heavenly Father will
also do to you if each of you does not forgive his brother from his heart.*

(HCSB)

Romans 7:19-23 & 8:1-5 –

*For I do not do the good that I want to do, but I practice the evil that I
do not want to do. Now if I do what I do not want, I am no longer the
one doing it, but it is the sin that lives in me. So I discover this principle: When I want to do what is good, evil is with me. For in my inner
self I joyfully agree with God's law. But I see a different law in the parts
of my body, waging war against the law of my mind and taking me
prisoner to the law of sin in the parts of my body.*

*Therefore, no condemnation now exists for those in Christ Jesus,
[2] because the Spirit's law of life in Christ Jesus has set you free from the
law of sin and of death. What the law could not do since it was limited by
the flesh, God did. He condemned sin in the flesh by sending His own
Son in flesh like ours under sin's domain, and as a sin offering, in order
that the law's requirement would be accomplished in us who do not walk
according to the flesh but according to the Spirit. For those who
live according to the flesh think about the things of the flesh, but those who
live according to the Spirit, about the things of the Spirit.*

(HCSB)

Ephesians 1:7-8 – "We have redemption in Him through His blood, the
forgiveness of our trespasses, according to the riches of His grace that
He lavished on us with all wisdom and understanding." (HCSB)

Read also Matthew 6:9-15 – The Lord's Prayer

UNDERSTANDING the SUMMATION

The world is full of people walking around impacted by their past. They have either wronged someone or been wronged by someone—or hurt by their own stumbles. They have built emotional walls, and bitterness has replaced kindness. Our culture does not urge forgiveness as the normal response when dealing with hurtful situations. Our society teaches us to get even or turn our backs. Our society is filled with broken, hurting people searching for happiness.

In the passage on the unforgiving servant, Matthew writes that Peter asked the Lord how many times should he forgive a brother who sins against him. Seven times? Jesus answers that it isn't as many as seven times, but seventy times seven times! Jesus told the parable of the unforgiving slave. The king shows this servant great compassion and cleared his debt after the slave dropped to his knees and begged for patience. However, the slave did not show this same compassion to his fellow slave.

What do you think hardened his heart to his fellow slave so much so that he choked him and threw him in jail? I'm sure he needed money to support his family, but his heart was blind to the plight of those in the same situation. Once the king heard of the slave's wickedness, he rescinded his kindness and tortured him until he paid. What an unfortunate turn of events for this man, all of which could have been avoided with one act of forgiveness.

We learn in Colossians that we are to forgive others just as the Lord forgives us. If we don't show kindness and compassion to forgive others, it will not be shown to us. Read the Lord's Prayer in Matthew 6 and the Scriptures following. We are to forgive others so our sins and wrongdoing will be forgiven. If it takes seventy times seven a day—or more!—

then that's what we must do for everyone. So too, then, it will be done for us.

It is logical to conclude that we cannot walk through our daily lives with unforgiveness in our hearts and expect God to freely offer His forgiveness to us. If we don't forgive, our hearts will become bitter and hard, not just towards the person who wronged us, but towards everyone and maybe even toward ourselves. Don't be like the slave who couldn't extend the same forgiveness to his fellow slave that was so graciously shown him.

In Ephesians, Paul taught us that we have redemption in Him through His blood and the forgiveness of our trespasses or wrongdoings according to the riches of His grace. Paul also wrote in Romans that he tried to do what was right, but his flesh would cause him to do the wrong thing. There was a war waging inside Paul. Paul was a godly man, sold out for God's cause, and yet he battled his flesh. He went on to write that no condemnation now exists for those in Christ Jesus. If we are saved, we are redeemed by Christ Jesus and can walk according to His Spirit, not our flesh.

No one is without sin except Jesus. Remaining in self-condemnation is not what God wants for us. We are children of the Most High, but we are going to make mistakes and fall short—after all, even the Apostle Paul battled his flesh. But we don't have to *stay there* and wallow in the flesh. Paul tells us that no condemnation now exists for those in Christ Jesus, because the Spirit's law of life in Christ Jesus has set us free from the law of sin and of death. He wants us to repent. We need to lay our sins at His throne, ask for forgiveness and move out of the flesh and into His forgiving spirit.

Really? Seventy times seven times! A day! I thought that was a bit excessive until I realized how many times the Lord has already forgiven me today. God sets the example of one who can truly love us and forgive us even though we don't deserve such compassion. If He can forgive me over and over again, then surely I can forgive myself over and over again. Surely I can forgive the person who stole my Mom's wedding ring and I can forgive anyone else who hurts me along the way. I, too, want my brother and sister to show me heartfelt kindness and compassion and forgive me. We should repent and seek forgiveness from God, accept that forgiveness, and show others that same compassion as a part of our daily walk with God.

Honestly, I didn't really want to forgive the person who stole my Mom's wedding ring. More importantly, I was and am supposed to be the example of Christian behavior for the rest of my immediate family and my extended family. I couldn't allow anger and bitterness to ruin my peace or my witness. The Lord says that if this person steals from me, or sins against me, seventy times seven times, I should forgive. I certainly can take steps to prevent theft; I don't have to let myself get walked on seventy times seven times, but I am called to forgive those who sin against me every time. I did forgive that person and prayed that she would find peace in the Lord.

GOD SHOWS US HEARTFELT COMPASSION, KINDNESS, HUMIL-ITY, GENTLENESS, AND PATIENCE MULTIPLE TIMES EVERY DAY. IF WE REALLY WANT TO FORGIVE LIKE JESUS, IT IS ONLY LOGICAL TO CONCLUDE THAT WE SHOULD SHOW THE SAME HEARTFELT COMPASSION AND FORGIVE OTHERS OVER AND OVER AGAIN.

God shows us heartfelt compassion, kindness, humility, gentleness, and patience multiple times every day. If we really want to forgive like Jesus, it is only logical to conclude that we should show the same heartfelt compassion and forgive others over and over again. God has already forgiven the person who stole the wedding ring. He's already forgiven the person who has wronged you, too. He's already forgiven you and me for the wrongs we commit on a daily basis. God's forgiveness gives us a chance to "redo" and get it right if we are truly repentant. It also seems logical that the words, "I forgive you" and "I am sorry" spoken seventy times seven times will allow healing for the pain that torments us and will bring down the walls that divide us. Together, we can make the norm in our society patience, humility, kindness, and heartfelt compassion.

I pray that you seek God's forgiveness now. Seek forgiveness from anyone you have wronged in the past. I pray that you cast all flaws or mistakes or miss-steps upon Jesus and forgive yourself as many times as necessary. Don't wallow in the flesh, but rise up in Christ's redeeming Spirit of forgiveness. I pray, also, that if you have unforgiveness in your heart for someone, ask God to show you how to forgive and let the healing begin. Use the words "I forgive you" and "I am sorry" often to free your spirit of bitterness and strife. I pray all of this in Jesus' name.

God is...my logical conclusion for forgiveness through Jesus.
Where are you seeking forgiveness?

Notes

MY ETERNAL LIFE

JOURNEY

Many times in my teens and twenties, I was asked the age-old question, "If I were to die tonight, do I think I would go to heaven?" My answer was, "I don't know; I sure hope so." Then, the following conversation would ensue: "I think I'm a good person; I certainly could be better. I'm nice to people. I donate items to worthy causes. I donate money sometimes. I volunteer occasionally. I'm no Mother Teresa, but I don't steal or kill. So, sure, I think I would go to heaven."

I was born and raised in the Catholic Church. I was baptized as an infant, celebrated my first communion in the second grade, and was confirmed in the ninth grade. I had a beautiful Catholic Mass at my wedding. I was taught the significance of missions, brotherly love, and tradition. I had recited many prayers and creeds over the years and confessed my faith in the church. My favorite priest dissected the Lord's Prayer for my confirmation class. He taught us the purpose behind each phrase. He showed us that the Lord's Prayer is a road map for every prayer. I remember his words today. I also carry with me the incredible reverence that was instilled in me for the sacrament of Communion. The Catholic Church is full of dear family and close friends.

However, my husband, John, was not Catholic. Although I had known him forever, when we married, I'm not sure he really knew my belief system or the Catholic belief system. We talked all around salvation, but not right at salvation. After we got married, we began searching for a new church home that would be a suitable compromise for us both. We found a small Lutheran Church that we attended for many years. During those early years, we began discussing heaven. In those discussions, John realized my "afterlife" dilemma. My dear, sweet husband bought me a Bible and showed me John 3:16. He shared with me that it was important that I confess my faith in Jesus as my Lord and savior. I had never known to take that step. I had never known that going to heaven depended on me taking that step. It was during that time when I did confess Jesus as my Lord and solidified my eternal life in heaven. My life has never been the same. In a few paragraphs I will share with you a simple confession of faith.

EXPLORING the STATUTES

John 3:16-17 – "For God so loved the world that He gave His one and only Son, that whoever believes in Him shall not die, but have eternal life. For God did not send His Son into the world to condemn the world, but to save the world through Him." (NIV)

Romans 10:9-10 – "If you confess with your mouth, 'Jesus is Lord,' and believe in your heart that God raised Him from the dead, you will be saved. One believes with the heart, resulting in righteousness and one confesses with the mouth, resulting in salvation." (HCSB)

Ephesians 2:8-9 – "For it is by grace that you have been saved, through faith, this is not from yourselves; it is the gift from God, not by works, so that no one can boast." (HCSB)

2 Timothy 1:9-11 "He has saved us and called us with a holy calling, not according to our works, but according to His own purpose and grace, which was given to us in Christ Jesus before time began. This has now been made evident through the appearing of our Savior Christ Jesus, who has abolished death and has brought life and immortality to light through the gospel." (HCSB)

1 Peter 4:2 – "As a result, they do not live the rest of their earthly lives for evil human desires, but rather for the will of God." (NIV)

Luke 3:3 – "He went into all the country around the Jordan, preaching a Baptism of repentance for the forgiveness of sins." (NIV)

1 Peter 3:21-22 – "This water symbolizes baptism that now saves you also- not the removal of dirt from the body, but the pledge of a clear conscience toward God. It saves you by the resurrection of Jesus Christ, who has gone into heaven and is at God's right hand." (NIV)

Read also – Romans 3:23, Romans 5:8, Romans 6:23, Romans 8:2, Romans 10:13, John 14:26

UNDERSTANDING the SUMMATION

I had always recited that Jesus was born of the Virgin Mary, was crucified for us, was put to death for our sins, and rose from the dead. What I knew of God was very much kept at an arm's length. I had not learned any Scriptures teaching of eternal life based on a confession and belief in *my* heart of Jesus as *my* Lord. I didn't know He died for *me* on a personal level. I thought it was more for *everyone* on a universal level.

I had never used the word "saved" or called Jesus my "Savior." I didn't know how to have a personal relationship with Christ.

The Scriptures listed above changed my thought process completely. I read these Scriptures and discussed them with my husband. It was interesting to me that John knew without a doubt that he was going to heaven. He had made a decision, with the help of his Mom, when he was nine years old. At nine years old, he believed in his heart and confessed Jesus as his Lord and Savior. At that moment, John secured his eternal life in heaven. At nine years old, he had the definitive answer to that age-old question. He could answer, "Yes, if I were to die tonight, I know I would go to heaven."

His answer was not based on what *he* had done. It was based on what he chose to believe about what *Jesus* had done for him on the cross. I wanted that answer, and obtaining it was simple.

One evening, I was sitting on my bed and I just started talking to God out loud. I said, "I believe that you sent your Son to die on the cross for me, I believe that He died and rose again. I confess that Jesus is my Lord." That was all there was to it. The earth didn't shake, and I didn't feel anything happen, but I knew something was different. I felt free. I was free from sin and death and condemnation. I wanted to tell someone, everyone. That's exactly what God wanted me to do.

I had already been baptized as an infant. I didn't feel the urge to run out and do it again, although I should have. I was baptized many years later with my son, which turned out to be a very special moment for me as a parent. Although Jesus never sinned, He set the example for all of us. John baptized him in the Jordan River. Baptism is a symbol of our sins being washed away, through the death and resurrection of Jesus Christ. It is more than just an act of going under water, but it represents a change of heart and a yearning for forgiveness through repentance—forgiveness that is freely given once we ask.

I began praying and seeking forgiveness for past indiscretions, and now I try to spend time praying and seeking forgiveness for daily mistakes. I didn't stop sinning or suddenly become perfect when I became a Christian, but now with the help of the Holy Spirit I am always improving and growing spiritually. Therefore, I believe that baptism does not get us into heaven, but baptism and repentance are part of God's plan to start our Christian walk down the right path.

Furthermore, God's Word says that we are saved by grace through faith and not by works. We are not going to heaven because we are good people, but rather because of God's grace and our belief and faith in the resurrection of Jesus Christ. This is a much better method of determining salvation, as gauging the number of good deeds necessary to gain access into heaven would be difficult and quite subjective. How "good" is good enough? We would live in constant fear of failure.

Know this one truth; Jesus did the work for us. His death on the cross was the sole act that opened the gates of heaven for our entry. He paid the ultimate price with His life, so that we don't have to live wondering and hoping that we are good enough. We never have to say, "I'm a good person. I hope I'm going to heaven. I hope I gave enough. I hope…." All we have to do is believe and confess Him as our Lord and Savior. Timothy said that Jesus saved us, not according to our works but according to His own purpose and grace.

> KNOW THIS ONE TRUTH; JESUS DID THE WORK FOR US. HIS DEATH ON THE CROSS WAS THE SOLE ACT THAT OPENED THE GATES HEAVEN FOR OUR ENTRY.

What path is the right path? I mentioned earlier that I knew something was different after I confessed Jesus as my Lord. God's Word also says in 1 Peter that we are not to live the rest of our lives for human desires but rather for God's will. However, it is only logical that God doesn't want us to gain salvation, then forget about Him and go on our merry way. He wants us to live according to His will and put our human desires to rest. We are called to know His will and His desires and live by a set of guidelines.

Knowing God can only come from spending time with Him in prayer and from learning His character and nature through His written Word. In John 14:26, Jesus tells us that the Counselor, His Holy Spirit, will be sent by the Father to teach us all things. We have a Holy Counselor to guide us as we navigate down life's path.

Some days, it's not easy to know what God wants us to do with our lives. Over the years, I have come to recognize the Holy Spirit guiding my thoughts. My awareness of His presence in my life has grown stronger and I have become more and more obedient. The right path has become easier to locate and His will easier to determine and follow.

It is my great honor to share with you the Scripture that my husband showed me—John 3:16, which so changed my life. God loves you so much that He sent His only Son, Jesus, so that everyone who believes in Him will not suffer eternal death but instead gain eternal life.

I pray that Jesus becomes your Lord and Savior.

I ask you, "If you were to die tonight, do you think you would go to heaven?" If you're not sure, but you want your answer to be yes, then, it is only logical that you first believe in your heart, and then confess these words:

God in heaven, I believe in my heart that you sent your one and only Son, Jesus, to die on the cross for me. I believe that He rose again. I confess that Jesus is my Lord, and I ask you to forgive me of my sins. I pray this in Jesus name. Amen.

I pray that you become aware of the Holy Spirit guiding your steps and never stop seeking the knowledge of God's will for your life. I encourage you to find a Bible-based church and experience the gift of baptism.

God's son, Jesus, is…my logical conclusion
for my Eternal Life and Savior.
Who is your Savior? Where is your Eternal Life?

Notes

MY LOGICAL CONCLUSION

In the earlier stages of writing this book, I offered a kind of challenge to God, "Okay, God, I will get off the bed and write, but I only have about a half a page rattling in my brain." I had no idea God would lead me down this path to these words on these pages in this format. Along the way, I caught myself both laughing and crying. With every word, I have learned more about myself and my God. I have been interrupted by a few short-term jobs in the oil industry here and there, none of them as exhilarating and fulfilling as writing these stories and sharing God's Word. I was always excited to get a chunk of time to sit at my computer and pour into these pages. The time would fly and day would turn into night. I have loved this process and felt God's Spirit speaking to me and flowing through me.

Once I took the first step, God opened the door to reveal the next step or few steps or sometimes even a flight of steps. I had to trust Him. It wasn't easy. Fear and doubt crept in frequently, and often I felt myself just want to give up and place this book on the computer "shelf" and never call the publisher. I have never done anything like this before. The words on these pages expose details of my life's story for everyone to read. Something inside continued to nudge my spirit to push through to completion.

Reaching the end of my life with the regret of not writing this book would break my heart. It would be the regret and heartbreak of disobeying God's request and ignoring His will for immeasurable fulfillment in my life.

During my lifetime, I have lost my dream of playing college basketball, my father, two pregnancies, and many jobs. I have cursed my marriage and my finances. I have learned that I am not perfect or in control. I have had to forgive and be forgiven…often. Through all of this, do you know what God has taught me? I'm doing okay.

In fact, I'm doing better than okay. Through this process, I met my Savior, who died on the cross to forgive my sins and give me eternal life. I also now know the One who is perfection and who developed the plan. I know the One who is my Healer, my Protector, and my Provider. I know peace that passes all understanding and a Father who shows love that never fails. I am a child of God and an heir to the throne equipped with the Word of God. It is logical to conclude that because I am abiding in Him, I am triumphant over all of the attacks that come my way.

I'm not a pastor or Bible scholar. I'm certainly not claiming to have all the answers, but I am willing to be used. God uses all the things in our lives and turns them to good for those who love Him. As I began writing this book, I was ready and willing for the next step, so now I ask you the big question:

Are you? I urge you to listen to that still small voice, take the first step, and embark on His journey for your life.

I challenge you to seek new heights in your spiritual growth. Dive deep into God's Word and meditate on its meaning. Determine to achieve excellence for His kingdom according to the gifts He has placed inside you.

As I have become obedient to God's calling on my life, spiritual doors have opened on so many levels. I have met Godly people and touched lives beyond anything I could have imagined. Because of my obedience, other people have made divine connections—connections that I never saw coming. God has a plan for so much more than we can see or imagine. If we don't listen and follow, He will use someone else, and our talent will be wasted.

Begin to visualize your role in this world with kingdom purpose and eternal impact. Believe that God has a plan for you that is greater than what is before you now. Know that you have significance in God's great scheme. Lean into His Word and the Savior and listen for His will to unfold. When you face a particular battle, don't seek worldly solutions; seek the Creator of the World. Turn to God's court, His throne and His Word. Become a doer of God's Word as James described in the following Scripture:

> But be doers of the word and not hearers only, deceiving your-selves, because if anyone is a hearer of the word and not a doer, he is like a man looking at his own face in a mirror. For he looks at himself, goes away, and immediately forgets what kind of man he was. But the one who looks intently into the perfect law of freedom and perseveres in it, and is not a forgetful hearer but one who does good works—this person will be blessed in what he does.
>
> James 1:22-25 (HCSB)

From the beginning, my mission was to bring God our Father and the words of the Bible down from this far away place in Heaven and into a place where you can meet Him, hear Him, and know Him. I hope I have achieved that mission. I hope that I have presented my Journey logically and showed you how Exploring the Statutes brings you to an Understanding of the Summation. I hope the JESUS Method becomes useful to enhance your Christian walk. Jesus is the logical conclusion for everything.

Psalm 46:10-11 God says, "Be still and know that I am God; I will be exalted among the nations, I will be exalted in the earth" (NIV). The Lord Almighty is with us.

Isaiah 9:6 informed us that, "For to us a child is born, to us a son is given, and the government will be on his shoulders. And He will be called Wonderful Counselor, Mighty God, Everlasting Father, Prince of Peace" (NIV).

And in John 14:27, Jesus said, "Peace I leave with you; my Peace I give you" (NIV).

> JESUS IS THE LOGICAL CONCLUSION FOR EVERYTHING.

The Scriptures above demonstrate God's mighty power. We must always recognize that He is God and exalted above all nations and above the earth. It is awesome to know that the Spirit of the Lord Almighty lives in us and is always guiding us. The Creator of the universe is our God, and we have the authority to live within that realm. He is our Wonderful Counselor, Mighty God, Everlasting Father, and Prince of Peace. I am believing for great revelations for you and a life of great breakthrough.

I pray that God will use this book and the JESUS Method to launch you into a deeper relationship with Him and a deeper knowledge of His Word. I pray that you become a doer of God's Word and walk down a path that is pleasing to Him. I also pray that you claim

your right as a co-heir with Jesus to God's throne and recognize your authority, as a child of the Most High, to access God's everlasting power and love.

God is...my logical conclusion for *everything*.
I pray my logical conclusion becomes yours.

Notes